BEHIND *my* SMILE

THE TRUE STORY OF AN AUTHOR, A BROKEN SPIRIT AND A HEALER

ALSO BY BERYL CROSHER-SEGERS
A Darker Shade of Pale: A Memoir of Apartheid South Africa

BEHIND *my* SMILE

THE TRUE STORY OF AN AUTHOR,
A BROKEN SPIRIT AND A HEALER

BERYL CROSHER-SEGERS

the kind press

Copyright © 2020 Beryl Crosher-Segers

First published by the kind press, 2020

All rights reserved. No part of this book may be reproduced, stored in a retrieval system or transmitted in any form or by any means, electronic, mechanical photocopying, recording, or otherwise, without written permission from the author and publisher.

This publication contains the opinions and ideas of its author. It is intended to provide helpful and informative material on the subjects addressed in the publication. While the publisher and author have used their best efforts in preparing this book, the material in this book is of the nature of general comment only. It is sold with the understanding that the author and publisher are not engaged in rendering advice or any other kind of personal professional service in the book. In the event that you use any of the information in this book for yourself, the author and the publisher assume no responsibility for your actions.

Cover and interior design by Elle Lynn
Editor: Shelly Kenigsberg
Author photos: Syl Marie Photography

Cataloguing-in-Publication entry is available from the National Library Australia.

NATIONAL LIBRARY OF AUSTRALIA

ISBN 978-0-6485917-6-4 (Paperback)
ISBN 978-0-6485917-7-1 (Ebook)

This book is dedicated to Geoff with my
deepest gratitude, for his kindness, encouragement,
healing and the many moments of pure magic.

ACKNOWLEDGEMENTS

BEHIND MY SMILE is a story born out of deep sorrow that took me on a journey of deep inward searching, searing pain and ultimately led me to immense peace about my earlier life. I gave the book this title because amidst the pain, I wore my smile like a mask.

To my publicist, Kristin Spiers, in Norway. I am so deeply grateful for your friendship and support. My life as an author changed completely when I met you. I am forever grateful for the many hours you have devoted to me not only as a client but as a friend and for everything you've done to get my work out into the world.

Thank you to my former editor turned publisher, Natasha Gilmour, from **the kind press**. Natasha, you are one of a kind. Our author/publisher/friend relationship has flourished as the years have gone by. I wish you and **the kind press** an amazingly successful journey in the publishing world. You've got this!

To my editor, Shelley Kenigsberg, my deepest gratitude for believing in my book, for believing in me, and for asking the right questions that helped me become a better writer. Without you this book would still be pages saved in my file. Your spirit and humour carried me through many challenging times to deliver this book. I will remain eternally grateful for this encounter. Not forgetting the active voice lessons!

To my parents, thank you for the gift of an education despite the odds stacked against us under oppression. I am eternally grateful to my Mum for her sacrifices during a tough life in apartheid South Africa. But she showed our oppressors what a strong mind is capable of. I know that my Dad will be so proud of my achievements.

My siblings, my life long companions — we are the inner circle. Nothing can break that, not even death.

To my 'wing person', my daughter Sasha, and granddaughters Chelsea and Charlotte. Thank you for loving me, for lifting my spirits, for all the girls' stuff, for making me roll with laughter and for all the dance moves. Mostly thank you for having my back.

To my son Michelin, Mr Logic himself, daughter-in-law Lisa, and grandchildren Joshua, Alexander and little Mia thank you for always surrounding me with love, encouragement and laughter. I cannot thank you both enough for upholding our family values of togetherness.

My deep gratitude goes to Dr Carlo Rinaudo and the team at the Brain Hub in Gladesville. You are my life savers. Carlo, I owe you so much for your guidance, expert care and for going beyond the call of duty to assist me. My toolkit is a memory of you that I carry around with me.

Thanks also to Dr Sue Joseph, lecturer in my Memory and Life Writing class for her guidance particularly with the prologue of this book. Thank you to all my lecturers, and fellow students for their encouragement in my daunting first semester at UTS.

To journalist, now political editor, Yoni Bashan whose input I valued particularly when I felt out of my depth back in a lecture room after such a long absence from formal study. Yoni, I will fondly remember our spirited discussions and your question: 'Where is your anger?' I hope my book reflects that very anger before my healing.

Thank you also to Dr Mark Cross who stepped into my realm unexpectedly and offered me immense opportunities. Me, the girl from the dusty township on the Cape Flats can now claim several pages in the book of a prominent psychiatrist. My father would be smiling. I am privileged and honoured to have you present the foreword in my book.

Words of appreciation fail me when I think of Dr Geoff Lyons, clinical psychologist and energy medicine practitioner. Geoff, what an honour and privilege to have worked with you during my mental health crisis. My healing journey, under your guidance, inspired this story. The therapy process was fraught with challenges but together we found a way forward through mutual respect and much empathy on your part. I will be forever grateful for the reason our paths crossed. It's time for you to come out of the shadows. Chapter 13's quote will forever be a reminder of the challenges!

To my family, friends, readers, followers and supporters around the world, a massive thank you. There are too many to mention by name. How wonderful is the age we live in where technology allows us to stay connected, to lift each other up and to offer support? My work would not be out in the world if not for your kindness. Many of you have lifted me higher than, I, at times thought possible.

To mental health sufferers everywhere, I urge you to find a healer. There is no need to suffer in silence. We are all each other's healers but first we must heal ourselves.

Finally, to my husband Chris, my first reader, listener, tea maker, encourager, maker of dreams come true and the man who owns my heart. Thank you for your unfailing tenderness in lifting my wings up whenever I falter.

THINGS TO KNOW ABOUT THIS BOOK

I'm not a medical professional. This is my personal and creative response to my condition, and the discoveries that led me through different healing modalities based on a broader set of techniques than are commonly found: a balance of modern science with traditional wisdom.

I have drawn on actual conversations with practitioners during therapy, with their permission. I am grateful for their willingness to trust me with their professional concepts as such openness is, in my experience, rare. Practitioners mentioned in this book[1] have helped me find direction and hope when I was in my deepest despair. Each has given me exceptional support and collectively they have given me boundless love, courage and strength and more.

---

[1] Dr Geoffrey Lyons, clinical psychologist and spiritual healer, Inspirit Psychology

Dr Carlo Rinaudo, chiropractor and neuro-vestibular practitioner, The Brain Hub.

TABLE OF CONTENTS

ACKNOWLEDGEMENTS		vii
THINGS TO KNOW ABOUT THIS BOOK		xi
FOREWORD		xv
PROLOGUE		1
CHAPTER 1	The book launch	7
CHAPTER 2	Confusion is my companion	19
CHAPTER 3	Healing, my search	27
CHAPTER 4	An unburdening begins	35
CHAPTER 5	How much longer?	41
CHAPTER 6	The healer	53
CHAPTER 7	Body and soul	69
CHAPTER 8	Cultivating peace	79
CHAPTER 9	Therapy, healing	87
CHAPTER 10	Quiet pain	103
CHAPTER 11	Brink of despair	115
CHAPTER 12	Next-level therapy	123
CHAPTER 13	Trauma, my broken spirit	133
CHAPTER 14	Grief, unspoken	145
CHAPTER 15	Outside of my power	157
CHAPTER 16	Feeling and healing	175
CHAPTER 17	And so, it is	185
ABOUT THE AUTHOR		190
WHERE TO FIND HELP		192

> *No tree, it is said, can grow to heaven unless its roots reach down to hell.*
>
> — CARL JUNG

FOREWORD

Beryl initiated contact with me via an email sent to my clinic rooms in September 2019. 'Good morning Dr Cross,' it so formally began, as I segue to this moment — writing a foreword for this powerful book on healing and light, written by an incredible person. A person with the amazing capacity to transform our relationship, in a journey of only four months, to one where we feel like kindred spirits. I wish we could say we are connected by shared ancestors, we may well be, but further back than both of us would prefer.

The email continued. 'I am the author of *A Darker Shade of Pale: a Memoir of Apartheid South Africa*. I've heard about your upcoming publication and the Big Anxiety Festival. My next book, *Behind My Smile*, deals with my battle with anxiety and panic disorder exacerbated by the release of my first book, and trauma suffered growing up in apartheid South Africa. I wanted to find out more about your publication and film.' So much evoked in that one paragraph, yet asking after me, and my projects; undemanding.

This is how connection and friendship pathways begin; by an act of email outreach, optimistically sent out in the ether. Only answered 3 weeks later by my then frazzled self just returned from a trip to the US, scrabbling to finish the very book that Beryl was asking me about. Culminating in a close bond, and me writing the foreword of this exquisitely frank account of Beryl's healing journey.

I have never read an account of therapy content so evocatively expressed before. Empathising with, is just not strong enough. I felt I was in the sessions with Beryl and Geoff, feeling Beryl's pain, as well as her strong connection with her spiritual guide and healer.

As a psychiatrist, I connect with the people who come to see me, not as some removed know-it-all, but as someone who explores the fragility of spirit and state of mind of those who seek help and healing. There has to be a therapeutic connection for any therapy to work. You have to believe in the professional, the expert, to whom you've entrusted the workings of your inner mind. But you are the real expert in terms of your life and meaning, including what you need in order to heal your trauma.

The healer is there to show you the way, but you have to tap into your core which includes your spirituality, your sense of connectedness to present and, also, to past. Faith, in the power of healing, and in the interaction with the person peeling away the layers until the heart of you is exposed, and ready to transform.

The reality of any trauma work is that for the person seeking healing, the only way to make sense of the hurt and pain, and heal, is by exposing the memories. You can no longer avert your gaze, nor deflect or suppress feelings any longer. You have to see, and acknowledge.

Trauma is so pervasive, its tentacular roots lodged in the firmament of one's core; a lifetime of coping strategies aimed at damage control or denial of its existence maintaining its choking hold.

By writing such a personal account of her childhood and early adult life, with past and ongoing trauma resulting in mental health issues, readers share Beryl's anger and anguish and her desire to heal.

A raw account of suffering is offered, invoking powerful responses in those receptive to its honest discourse. And her triumph — a rising above the hate, allowing the pain of loss and shame to be released. Release is powerful, but trauma doesn't follow set rules, it doesn't flow out of the mind in gentle undulating waves. It renders you vulnerable, and open to self-doubt and hurtful self-talk that you would never use against another human being. Who needs enemies when you have your crushed and self-blaming inner critic doing such a great job? It also opens you up to attack by those lurking in the Internet.

Trolls beware. Stay under your rocks, or be blinded by love and truth.

Beryl clearly articulates her hurt, the visceral response to such attacks, for this is what they are, in no uncertain terms. Anger, boiling up, heated by the fires of oppression, lashing out, uncontained. Retreat, isolation, resultant confusion in loved ones, furthering shame and self-blame. A story so common on my therapy chair as to make me want to wail and weep at what we humans do to each other.

Brave Beryl, for that is what she is, bearing down, not backing away, reaching out and being heard. A true woman of Africa.

A therapeutic relationship is a private one, no one external is usually privy to the interaction between therapist and client. The description of the therapy process in this book is frank, visceral, tangible. Beryl has shared herself, her intimate journey, so eloquently phrased, so exquisitely detailed, with us. To allow such scrutiny is brave and inspiring, which is how I so describe Beryl and Geoff.

As a fellow shrink, I strive to break down barriers, to destigmatise as well as humanise, those with mental health issues. Allowing such a journey to be shared in a book, takes both courage and spirit.

We operate in a clinical world where notions of maintaining impermeable boundaries are concrete, coupled with the fear of professional approbation or censure if you share of yourself with your therapy clients. This is not the definition of a true healing process, nor one I am interested in.

Opening emotional floodgates, then pointing to the time, with an admonishment to, 'Hold that thought till next week,' is not therapy.

Showing compassion and kindness, instilling faith and the feeling of being both held and heard, is. Empowering people between sessions, allowing interaction and communication between each formal weekly hour, takes commitment, care, positive synergy and, most importantly, passionate regard of other.

Unforced or responsive touch, whether by hug or hand on shoulder, or figuratively on someone's heart, can be part of that process; without denoting menace, or crossing boundaries.

Knowing that what you share with the therapist will not overwhelm them. That you are whole, buoyed by the spirits of your ancestors, the connection you have with your Gods and Mother Earth, accompanying and guiding your renovation of spirit.

I applaud Geoff, for being so open and allowing us in, into his private working space, vulnerable to critique. Not many therapists would have done the same, indeed some of those to whom Geoff turned for guidance and support vehemently opposed the idea. Geoff, I am glad you ignored that advice.

You have guided a beautiful transformative healing narrative.

In so doing, you've shown us that compassion, care, humanity and spirituality belong in the healing embrace of therapy. That we, as therapists, can at times remove the protective armour of our professional standing and reveal ourselves. We can forge a healing bond with those who visit us, one that is genuine. Real healing takes place when people work together, in a safe space, unencumbered by fear of judgement, or shame.

I read Beryl's acknowledgements for this book, one being that her father would be so proud of her being included in a book written by a psychiatrist, namely me. Never mind that the same psychiatrist — a lighter shade of pale, neurotic boy from the South African burbs who still can't quite believe that people actually listen to what he has to say — is in awe of his daughter and her life journey, and honoured to be invited to do so.

We thank you, Beryl and Geoff, for caring enough to bring this powerful journey to the light.

Dr Mark Cross, consultant psychiatrist, Northside Group Sydney, and SANE Australia board director. Co-author, with Catherine Hanrahan, of *Changing Minds, The go-to Guide to Mental Health for Family and Friends*, HarperCollins, 2016, and author of *'Anxiety': Expert advice from a neurotic shrink who's lived with it all his life*, HarperCollins, 2020.

PROLOGUE

WHAT'S HAPPENING TO ME? Am I dying?

It's the middle of the day and the lounge room is hazy despite the sun streaming through the windows. The room is spinning. The wooden floor offers some grounding. I'm struggling to focus as I look across the open plan into the kitchen.

Breathe.
Slow it down. Breathe in, hold, and breathe out.
Count, it'll help slow rapid heartbeat.
I can't swallow. Why is my tongue stuck to my palate?
I must crawl to the sink.
Are those worms under my skin? I can't lift my arms. Don't pass out, don't pass out … help is coming.
The siren.
Yes, I called the ambulance.
I'm dying.

CHRIS MUST BE FRANTIC. I couldn't tell him on the phone what was wrong. In the last few months, he has struggled to cope with me being in pain. He'd never doubted my strength or courage — I was the tough one, the person who most men were wary of when they made an inappropriate comment.

'Get your wings up,' he'd say whenever I faltered. And I would stand tall again, and raise my wings, ready to soar into the next challenge. I loved being challenged, loved being the strong one in my family.

But in this moment, I needed him. I had to stem the loss of energy that had been seeping through the cracks in my armour.

What has happened to my iron shirt?
I have no shield.
Oh God, let me live, I don't want to die on this floor. I don't want to die alone.

IN THE EARLY HOURS OF THAT MORNING, I had sat in my safe place – on the bathroom floor.

I should have been the happiest person alive. I had finally achieved my lifelong dream to write and publish a book. Yet? The painstaking years of hard work — deep inward searching, tears, edits, self-doubt, rewrites, fear — had left me drained. Many times, walking away from writing, from facing these memories, held so deeply inside, was the only option.

But the book is my dream. And when the words flow, the tears flow.

WHOSE REFLECTION IS THIS IN THE MIRROR?
My skin, is dull and pale; my lifeless eyes shift from the mirror to the tablets on the shelf. My face scares me.
I'm so tired.
In the harsh light the tiles look ugly.
We need a new bathroom. For a while, curled up on the mat resting my back against the bath, I start counting. First the floor; then the wall. We have forty-two floor tiles and 129 wall tiles.

What's happening? Nothing much has changed since last week. But from as far back as I can remember, it's been the same; the churning in my stomach, like a whirlpool. It leaves me gasping, trying to suck in the air.
I'm sinking, the water covers my face.
I'm drowning.

THE EVENTS OF THE LAST FEW MONTHS have shaken me intensely. I can no longer fake an interest in the praise, laughter and chattering around me. I'm struggling to process my success and grappling with the fact that others want to read, and are reading, my book. This book — written in the privacy of my study, just me and my memories — is my life and now, that's under scrutiny. I've been stripped of my dignity and placed in a blazing spotlight.

Who am I? Where do I come from? How did I write this book?

'Who are you to write this book?'

'What did you do for the anti-apartheid movement?'

Crushing thoughts. I need an escape to my own sacred place, deep in the solace of my mind. Somewhere to cradle the memories, feel them, touch them and, also, wish some of them away.

Now, in the darkness, my spirited opinions and views are in silence. Nothing interests me. A pile of books on my side table has been unopened for weeks.

I don't know where to go from here. I'm so afraid of crossing into the darkness.

I'M ON THE WOODEN FLOOR in the lounge searching the pictures on the wall for a familiar face. I can't see anyone. When the paramedics arrive, I sense they know what is wrong, but don't say it. They help me off the floor, chat calmly and check my vital signs. I struggle to hear what they were saying. My chest is labouring under my rapid heartbeat and my muscles, are vibrating, pushing my anxiety throughout my body.

My voice is barely a whisper. '*Am I dying?*'

'Can you tell us what happened?'

'I'm not sure. I feel sick.'

'Are you on any medication?'

'No.'

My eyes remain fixated on the equipment.

'Everything is normal and that's good,' they reassure me.

Outside I hear Chris's car screech to a halt and his footsteps pound to the front door. He'll save me. He always does.

THREE TIMES THIS MONTH I've been admitted to hospital and kept under observation because of my racing heart and trembling body. I've been told it is part of an anxiety and panic disorder. This year it has been at its worst.

Over the years I've managed my anxiety in many ways. Mainly by shutting out my fears and plunging into any project without any regard for my ability to cope.

In the hospital observation ward, after the episode in my lounge, the registrar sat on my bed and looked at me sympathetically. He had, no doubt, seen in my records that this was the third time I'd been admitted this month.

His calmness is comforting. He hands me some printed sheets and encourages me to read them. The heading says, Postural Orthostatic Tachycardia Syndrome (PoTS).

I want to tell him what is happening inside; my fears, my recurrent nightmares, especially the one where I am drowning. That, I know, is one of the reasons for my rapid and fluctuating heart rate. But I can't find the words. Instead, I take the papers he offers and start reading to hide my tears.

I started reading about the symptoms — lightheadedness, fainting and rapid heartbeat, usually triggered when a person stands up after lying down. They're relieved by lying down again. My over-thinking brain immediately matches the symptoms.

Soon I start fearing there's another unknown medical condition. This fear builds up behind my eyes, spreads across my face, and raises my heart rate so wildly that it leaves me gasping for air. 'Stand, rock, sit, squirm,' my anxiety orders.

How can I tell him my mind is so out of control? That anxiety is coursing through my body and ruling my thoughts. *I'm ashamed to tell him about my book, or explain online trolls and grief and the trauma?* They'll put me in an asylum and I'll wander around in a drug-induced stupor. I don't want a mental health problem or medication. That happens to others not to me.

This time, the registrar keeps me overnight.

Outside the sun will soon go down and the dancing shadows will grow longer. In the hours and minutes in the darkness of night, the dreams will come. Sleep will evade me. The water will submerge my body. I'll struggle to breathe. I've been here many times. I'm so tired of these fears.

After my younger brother Owen drowned, I was plagued by his sudden disappearance from our lives. I was very frightened about being separated from my family. Each time I saw his eyes, in the small framed photo in the loungeroom, they followed me. I was terrified about not being able to swim and of drowning. I have been plagued by nightmares ever since.

Can someone help me fix this please?

At home I would have wandered around the house, or spent time writing, to calm myself. Conscious not to alarm Chris, or my daughter, Sasha, and son, Michelin, I chose silence. Shut my eyes tightly and wished it away. I had become an expert at hiding my pain.

On discharge the hospital refers me to a cardiologist for investigation regarding PoTs.

That night, careful not to wake Chris, I slide out of bed to the bathroom. What I see in the mirror startles me. My eyes, weak and dull, squint against the harsh light. The reflection of the light on the bath, vanity and tiles hurts my eyes. The tiles look so ugly.

I count tiles again. Forty-two floor tiles and 129 wall tiles. Nothing has changed.

So, I write. Writing distracts me and calms my racing thoughts. It always does. In the study, my fingers tap away until morning light flickers through the blinds.

All is well again.

MUCH TO MY RELIEF, the cardiologist rules out PoTs. I read my medical notes, and see the hellish events of the last few months entered onto the hospital records. But anxiety and panic attacks are not new to me. I was born anxious.

The worst part of my disorder is that I'm fully aware it is irrational and often inexplicable, yet knowing that is no help when I am on that rollercoaster. It usually deepens the anxiety when I realise the signs. If I know it's irrational, *why… why can't I stop it?* The out of control feeling increases my fear. So, often, I begin fearing fear. I start anticipating panic attacks and at times manifest them. *Oh God, I can't stop it.*

My anxiety and I have an uncanny relationship, it controls my mind, tricking me into believing that I'll fail and disaster looms. A spiral of personal failure. Despite the many opportunities that have come my way, the dream jobs, living my best life in terms of high-profile events, travelling the world, there is the constant self-doubt and a battle against my anxiety. Thoughts, destructive and persistent, slam my self-esteem.

I am not good enough. I certainly don't deserve success. If I don't succeed, I'll be letting people down.

I'm on a continual search for improvement, as well as to proving I can do things better, bigger, than others. The endless need to shine; a trait I developed while living under oppression. I had to show them, the privileged, that I could be like them. That we are the same and not the downtrodden as they make us believe. I need to make plans. I tackle projects that will make me look successful even when I lack the resources. From my small home office, I derived great satisfaction in creating projects that allow others to shine. But I no longer feel like the strong smiling woman everyone knows me as or the one they expect me to be.

Despite things feeling normal for a few days, my anxiety and associated problems continue to affect my mental and physical health. On top of a diagnosis two years earlier of benign paroxysmal positional vertigo (BPPV), which manifests in episodes of severe spinning, blurred vision, dizziness and poor balance, my mental health continued to deteriorate.

I've faced challenges for many years. But now, I'm about to face some of the biggest challenges of my life to get well again.

CHAPTER ONE
THE BOOK LAUNCH

Everybody now admits that apartheid was wrong, and all I did was tell the people who wanted to know where I come from how we lived in South Africa.
I just told the world the truth. And if my truth then becomes political, I can't do anything about that.

— Miriam Makeba

WHEN I LAUNCHED MY MEMOIR, *A Darker Shade of Pale*, I felt wonderful. I was busy with book talks and media interest was high and it was all demanding. But hey, I felt invincible. I owned my power.

How wrong I was.

My story — a story I dearly wanted to tell — has its roots in apartheid-era South Africa. I wanted future generations to know the rich culture they stemmed from. Know, too, how fraught and, even, devastating that world was.

Growing up on the Cape Flats, a batch of townships for those classified as 'coloured' by the reigning National Party, I knew only one world. I didn't know there was a richer life on the other side of the bushes that surrounded our scrubby land, an alternative dimension on the other side of a railway line. White children were living privileged lives and I was oblivious. As a kid, I even thought apartheid life was normal. How wrong I was. But age soon brought a jolt of awareness that was to rattle my world.

MY BOOK HIT NUMBER ONE on Amazon Australia in several categories sparking media interest both in Australia and in South Africa. It coincided with celebrations for Nelson Mandela's 100th birthday and further media interest in South Africa's journey to freedom.

I know I'm an expert in my own story, but being drawn into discussing the current political situation in South Africa was something I didn't want to get embroiled in. My 'non-comment' unsettled the online opinion. '*Apartheid is dead,*' they said. '*But what's your opinion of the mess democracy has created? What's important now is the disadvantage for white people.*'

The tone of it frustrated me, hurt. I'm speaking of our history to remind ourselves not to inflict such pain, hardship, racism on anyone else, ever. It's an issue that always evokes strong emotions. The most potent is a deep anger and resentment towards those who were my oppressors.

Knowing and telling our stories is an important way for us to heal ourselves, to teach, and remind, a new generation where they've come from and what they can choose to be, now. Even when the dominant stories are horrific, but especially when they are hopeful, they can be stories of survival that shape our lives and preserve family history. We are characters in our own stories, and can shape our plotlines to win the day.

While my book received praise from many, for others it reopened old wounds. Tales and evidence of the harsh brutality meted out by privileged white South Africans resurfaced on my blog and my social media pages. My story was an uncovering of the extent and specifics of damage meted out by those with privilege and there was a virulent and, unexpected, backlash.

The responses and opinions from some South Africans that surfaced on my social media seemed to be the voices of the previously privileged; it seemed that white supremacy flourished still and that change in power had given vent to vile, scorching comments, and even threats.

Without a way to respond to these remarks, I still wanted to rebuff our oppressors; put paid to the burning hurt. It was those who controlled our lives, who installed this dark regime who deserved the scorn.

The personal attacks were a daily intrusion. After news.com.au published an interview where I articulated the brutality of apartheid, the attacks increased. Threats of finding my residential address and organising a protest surfaced on social media. Personal attacks on my lineage and other derogatory remarks intensified. Evil wishes for my ill-health and that of my family, dismissive remarks about my credibility. All of it when I doubted any had even read the book.

'Go back to South Africa. Australia does not want traitors like you,' one hissed.

'You are made up of a bit of this and a bit of that, that is why you are so messed up,' said another.

'Go back so the blacks can rape you.'

Desperate to shield my family from the brunt of these attacks, I withdrew, in silence. My husband, Chris, became increasingly concerned about the impact this was having on me. I was hyper-vigilant and my anxiety soared. I had no effective way of defending myself against these invisible attackers, trolls sitting behind their screens airing their brutal views. My mental state declined very quickly. These weren't comments about my writing, or my storytelling. This was personal.

When I was asked to talk about the book, I felt increasingly compelled to remind those who inflicted apartheid on us, what they owed us. I'm committed to help them not only understand and own their privilege but to turn it to some good use. Their privilege came at our disadvantage.

What matters to me is talking about and understanding the history and its effects. Attacking me about the book serves no purpose.

The commentators' agenda seemed designed to shift the focus. Away from responsibility and on to blame. To attack me for speaking about what life for me, my family, my community was like under apartheid. Life. They brandished me unworthy of an opinion They ridiculed my story as ancient history, something that needed to be buried without a trace.

They wanted to talk about the current situation in South Africa, particularly in relation to murders of white farmers. That's not what I was talking about; it's certainly not something I condone. Violent retribution in any form is unforgivable. But for the trolls, our disadvantage was undeserving of a mention in South Africa's history.

Still, the history stands. Our parents, my generation, were paid slave wages. We lost properties; we were excluded from certain jobs. The government paid 38 times more to educate a white child than a 'coloured' child. Our education in the townships was under-funded and second grade. Still today, families in the townships all over South Africa live in poverty, with little chance of moving out of that cycle.

THEN, MY MIND WENT INTO OVERDRIVE, consumed with avenues to confront my critics as a common theme from their comments emerged. It seemed easier for many privileged to merely say they couldn't change the past, than to take responsibility for the oppressive legacies. To admit that while they benefited it was detrimental to the marginalised.

Today, it's vital, to make a positive contribution; a difference. That is what I wanted my readers to think about. I have met a few ex-South Africans, now living in Australia, who work tirelessly to serve the poorest of the poor. These people are fine examples of what humanity is about. Instead of these trolls tearing me apart, there were many projects that they could focus on to improve the lives of their fellow South Africans. There are ample opportunities to compensate the disadvantaged.

DESPITE KNOWING ALL THAT, my speaking engagements for the year became increasingly hard to deliver. I still wanted to deliver the message about the brutality of apartheid and inform those who knew little about our history. I was continually surprised at how many didn't know the details, even if they knew the term 'apartheid'. I wanted the message of our pain and suffering to never be forgotten and never inflicted on anyone, ever again. I had a crystal-clear statement that apartheid was depraved, dehumanising, evil, ugly, violent. It was indefensible.

'I HEARD YOU SPEAK a few months ago and your down-to-earthness impressed me then,' a guest said when she approached me after an event, where I was a guest speaker. I was, first, pleasantly surprised. Then, stunned.

'Now however, I must say, you have lost your humility.' She was admonishing me for my speech. She appeared uncomfortable, even offended, that I referred to apartheid as horrendous.

Behind the scenes I was crumbling under the pressure of delivering these talks and reliving the life I'd left behind. It's true that I wanted remorse of some sort from those who benefitted from privilege over me. But in recalling my day-to-day humiliations the trauma had resurfaced. Now in this country, this person and I are friends, but growing up we could never have been friends.

Though my father had drummed into us that we were just as good as anyone else, white society — white South Africa — was telling us a different story, as loudly as it could. Its narrative, however, went beyond words to real actions of cruelty and subjugation.

Why was this the case? My life in South Africa was mapped out to a large extent; determined by the fact I was mixed race. My father, born on the island of Saint Helena on the west coast of Africa, was of East Indian heritage; my mother is Portuguese and Mozambican. This made me not white enough to enjoy the privileges of the 'superior race'— yet I was spared being banished to the black homelands to live in squalor.

Instead, my classification removed me from both black and white. It meant I would grow up in sub-economic housing in areas separate from both black and white, in areas that reeked of failure and deprivation.

I was 19 before I realised the truth. I write about that epiphany, that moment when I first saw how my family, friends and many fellow citizens were trapped in a toxic system.

We were brainwashed to accept fines for sitting in the wrong carriage on trains or for sitting on benches. Nothing subtle about racism in South Africa. Signs on buses, on placards, on buildings told us where we could or could not go. Signs ensured we were barred from sitting in anything other than our allocated places for fear of the consequences.

We grew up with the toxic, subliminal and stated inferiority of our race. And the complex was drilled into us by South Africa's powerful, white storytellers, who said, 'You are not the same as we are; you are inferior.' We were always on guard. Spies in our own lives. Checking myself to see if I was sitting on the correct bench, or walking through the right entrance.

I grew up feeling I had to be white to be successful. When you're forced to aspire to be someone else to survive you can lose touch with who you truly are.

Now, through the book, I had a voice, but almost 25 years after freedom in South Africa, there were ex-South Africans, the privileged, who still wanted to diminish what I'd said; to even disavow what had happened to me.

IT WAS IN CAPE TOWN on Monday 30 April 2018, at my book launch at Retreat Library where my trauma worsened. The day before, I had had a successful, warm and welcoming book launch at Kaleidoscope Café, generously supported by the owners, Glenn and Michelle Robertson. The engaged audience, expressing their admiration for my achievement raised me to heights I'd never have imagined. Musicians provided the afternoon's entertainment.

I chatted excitedly with the indomitable journalist, Dougie Oakes, who'd offered me immense support and encouragement during my writing journey.

As a child, it was in this Retreat Library that I found my only source of entertainment and solace. It was the one place where I could fill my senses with stories even if most of these stories were of children living privileged lives. All the characters in our books had blonde hair and blue eyes. They didn't resemble us. Even the drawings I made as a child depicted that same look. Still, I loved the library.

The library, now in a new location, was larger than it had been with a larger collection of books as well as improved facilities. I chose the venue for my launch as a reminder of my childhood and because I wanted to be close to the community in which I grew up. Retreat was also the home of a fellow high school student, the Distinguished Professor Jonathan Jansen. It felt like a homecoming.

Soon the library foyer was abuzz with guests arriving. My skin, had started crawling and itching and I reached down to my legs to scratch. Slowly, a tingling began in my arms and legs and my breathing grew more rapid. For a few moments, the room looked hazy. But instead of running to the bathroom to count tiles, I froze.

Just breathe, walk to your seat, this will soon be over.

When Jonathan arrived, people crowded around him while we posed for the obligatory photographs and smiles. Jonathan, who grew up in the same disadvantaged community, is a revered role model. His presentation, the smiling faces of my cousins and a few familiar faces kept me focused. School friends and former neighbours beamed from the audience. When the audience was given time to ask questions, there was an intense response. I had reopened old wounds, so this was somewhat expected.

While there were many from the 'born free' generation in the audience — those born after the end of apartheid — the prevalent topic was how people could move forward from the past. This is something that plagued many at different stages of their lives. This trauma surfaces, at times, when we least expect it.

As I sat next to Jonathan, my smile firmly in place, I struggled to keep my breathing in check. From the back of room, leaning against the wall came a face from my past. I didn't recognise him at first; it had been more than 40 years since I last saw him.

But I could hardly concentrate on the questions because at any moment he could step forward to embarrass me by asking a question. Thankfully he remained motionless at the back of the room.

A few minutes earlier, in the foyer, he'd greeted me like an old friend. Only he came armed with an invisible shovel and I imagined him starting to dig, deep and, with each movement, exposing layers I had so worked hard and carefully to cover up. The digging revealed what I thought was a healed wound. But his look was odd and, somehow, frightening. Within moments, I was filled with a crippling fear and felt the urge to go to the bathroom, splash my face and calm down.

'Congratulations on your memoir.' He smiled as he walked up to me. 'You're putting the suburb of Steenberg on the world map. I read your book. What a story! Though, you know there's one thing missing. I thought you'd write about what happened all those years ago. Remember?' He was taunting me. 'When that teacher came to your house that morning. I mean, there was a rumour he found you asleep in bed. But what really happened in your bedroom that morning?'

In an instant I was back at school, the sound of the sneering and laughter echoing in my ears. The teacher he referred to was one of our most dedicated and respected educators who went beyond the call of duty to help us reach our potential. It was an ugly slur on the teacher's reputation as well as mine. At that time, there was no one to protect me from these tormentors. My older siblings, Frances and George, had finished high school. I was on my own. I didn't know how to tell my Mum or Dad about this. I was a loner at school and spent my time writing and observing; I thought it made me almost invisible. But the ugly comments and innuendo were always loud enough for me to hear.

My school work suffered and I withdrew from everyone. No one noticed that I was spending more time on my own, forever scribbling notes. Mum worked six days a week from sunrise to sunset. Thoughts of escaping the torture consumed me. But there was no escape; I had to return to school every day.

This was hard. I had been here many times before.

'This is what memoirs are about, spilling the saucy beans,' he continued. 'We all know there was more to the story. You, Miss Goody Two Shoes, Miss Prim and Proper, always quiet, hey? The picture of innocence. Why didn't you, you know, tell all? That would have made for good reading. Now you are so grand, an Australian, living the glamorous life. Are you here to look down on us Miss Haughty?'

I looked at him and said nothing.

Thankfully, I was distracted by people standing around wanting to greet and take photographs. In a flash he had moved away inside the room. Shakily, I smiled and greeted people.

When he walked away, he left an area so raw that it felt as if it had been waiting for years to burst. I was scared again. I was only 15 years old when I became the victim of gossip and ridicule at school. I was ostracised and discarded like a dirty rag. But it was an experience I'd buried till then.

Jonathan spoke enthusiastically about my book and what purpose our stories would serve our community. He marvelled at my memory and the detail I provided. He sang my praises as a storyteller. This should have been a proud moment. I had dreamed of being recognised as a writer for decades. But I felt lost, my confidence had been shaken. I couldn't absorb what was being said.

Can someone help me, please?

At the end of his launch, we had a conversation about the difficult years under apartheid, about my author journey. It helped me remain focused on the subject because I was conscious of the significance of the occasion. I forced myself to remain in the moment. This was my time. Yet, no matter how much I tried, it seemed to all be crashing down around me.

But look at the crowd that's here.

So many faces smiling at me. This diverse gathering was of friends as well as people from the 'other side' of the line. White people sitting in our library in our hood. This was new to me. The event had booked out a few weeks prior, and there was standing room only for late comers. I couldn't have imagined the support I'd get from the community.

AS THE QUESTIONS FROM THE AUDIENCE CONTINUED, while I wrestled with my fear, I knew the signs: squirming in my seat, my anxiety would soon escalate into panic. I willed myself to slow my breathing, and stop the panic building up in my limbs and face. I gulped some water to wet my mouth. My eyes frantically searched for Chris.

Just breathe, you'll get through this.

Then, without my saying anything more, the presentation was over. My childhood friends came up to talk. People were lining up for the book signing so we could only briefly hug and greet. With promises to catch up over the next few days, they were gone. I had had so much to say to them.

Still, there was a figure at the back distracting me.

CHRIS WAS IN HIS ELEMENT, socialising, catching up with friends unaware of my desperate signal for help with wrapping up the night. He didn't notice the urgency in my eyes.

That night, back in our room at the guesthouse, my anxiety was at breaking point and into full blown panic. Adrenaline cursed through my body like a rush of agitated water filling every cell. Through the pain, my voice roared like a wounded lion into the darkness. I paced around the room, unable to control the shaking. My breathing was so rapid that my body movements jerked out of control. Chris insisted we go to the nearest hospital.

My cousin Yvette and her husband, Edward, our gracious hosts, took us to Emergency. They sat in the hospital waiting room, offering support but unaware of my mental fatigue. The fear of showing this weakness to anyone was too overwhelming.

The doctor who, immediately administered a tranquiliser, encouraged me to relax; urged me to enjoy my time in the country. What bliss it would have been to calm down and go back to bed. I could not sleep; there was still one book signing to go.

CHAPTER TWO
CONFUSION IS MY COMPANION

One can't erase the tremendous burden of apartheid in 10 years, 20 years, I believe, even in 30 years.

— Susan Rice

THE EXCITEMENT OF BEING IN MY BIRTH TOWN had lost its glow. A hospital visit was not part of the plan. But I had come back to the guest house and tried to rest. Whenever I fell asleep, I dreamed my body, submerged, would violently splash around to keep afloat.

The traumatic night had unravelled all the trauma of my past, allowed my daily humiliations to flood back. Monsters had surfaced and those carefully buried events now oozed out of a gaping hole.

Sitting at breakfast, I had to make quick dashes to my bedroom to ease my panic. If the others noticed my unease, they didn't show it. They continued lavishing me with love and attention.

My cousins Dawn, Gail, Günther and Karen came to visit. It was a long awaited catch up with Günther, planned months earlier while I was in the throes of writing and he was helping with fact-checking. Finally, face-to-face, signing copies for my family, my smile, albeit weak, broke through.

Still, this was not the picture it was supposed to be. I was in Cape Town, the town of my birth, a place where I was known;

where I'd party from sunrise till all hours.

Now I was holed up in my room hiding from the world. Screwed up. Lacking the tools to dig myself out of this hole. The familiar home food that I so longed for in Australia, remained untouched on my plate. I needed the safety of my own home and surroundings, my place to hide.

On one of my dashes to get away, Dawn followed me to the room.

'Are you OK?' she asked.

'Not sure what's happening but I'm so… so anxious,' I said. 'I haven't slept much since we got here.'

I longed to unburden my fears, my frustrations, cry. She offered me some calming medication and, in desperation, I gulped down a couple of tablets. I took some to keep for the night. I wanted tomorrow to be different. I wanted to enjoy the city, catch up with family and friends. But a darkness followed me everywhere.

We'd taken a drive through the area where I grew up and it had unsettled me even further. I could see poverty, the desperation on people's faces and, when I spoke to people, it upset me to hear the hopelessness in their voices.

I'd run around in these hills; played in the streets, lived where neighbours knew and cared for each other. Now, roads were empty, people hidden behind security doors and high walls. The violence and threats of it, meant raising families amid the daily sounds of gunshots. Many died on the streets. I felt this pain. My heart went out to ragged children walking the streets. The legacy of apartheid was still so evident.

We had several days before our flight home but my fatigue had escalated. I'd force myself to go for walks on the picturesque Blouberg beach along the Indian ocean close to the guesthouse. At night, my nightmares were at their worst. One night when I woke up wet with perspiration, I looked up the contact details of South African Airways in Sydney to see if I could get home on the next flight. When Chris woke, I announced we could get on a flight home that day. I had to get home.

WRITING HAS BEEN MY ESCAPE since my teens. So many conversations stored in the pages in my brain. Sometimes, when the darkness sets in and I open those pages the conversations have frozen. Many of those pages bore a deep pain and an unrelenting shame. And they wouldn't be closed.

In *A Darker Shade of Pale*, I was open and honest about my life. Writing it was a heartfelt, difficult but vital way to heal my past; to encourage others to do the same. Some of the writing was fuelled by my father's voice condemning the dehumanising conditions we'd been relegated to. After his death, many of the things he cursed the government for, started to make more sense and began to infuriate me. As I grew older, my anger and frustration grew more fierce.

As I promoted the book through speaking events engaging with the media, on social media platforms and a new public, I was also revisiting memories lodged in my spirit. Wounds were reopened and a deep pain was with me. Constantly. In some places, wounds started festering. The scabs were itching to come off.

As the weeks progressed, there were many heart-warming messages from readers, baring their souls about their own stories of survival. There were encouraging reviews and congratulatory messages.

Alongside those, some members of the public started sending intimidating messages about my book. Online trolls attacked wherever my book was promoted on social media. I was confused, angry, shattered but, mostly, utterly unprepared for the aftermath of publication.

The assaults were relentless. a few were accusing.

'You ran away while we stayed to fight for the rainbow nation' people said. Many were downright heartless and insulting.

The poison arrows found their mark and I dropped into a dark pit and sometimes, I languished in my bed for days. On days I managed to climb out of the hole, someone would take the liberty of shoving me back down. Graphic images of dead bodies, blood baths and horrific injuries appeared when I opened mail about the book. Evil statements surfaced accusing me of inciting a white genocide. There was nothing subtle about the hate speech directed at me. Messages of, 'Go back to South Africa, you kaffir lover,' slashed my screen.

Though I was safe, at home, my anguish reverberated and I was terrified to leave home or be alone. Being in public places or, even, being caught at a red traffic light heightened my anxiety to full blown panic. I couldn't bear communicating face-to-face. More and more I sought the safety of my bedroom. I grew so furious at the ugly messages coming through that I wanted to hit out at these invisible people. All the while, that went against so much of what I believed in; what I'd been taught as a child.

For my parents, respect for our fellow humans was paramount. I understood we are capable of deep emotions. For many of us, empathy, love for one another, courage, and peace are the cornerstones of our existence. I'd sustained my belief in this, my trust, for generations.

But now these emotions also revealed our ability to hurt, to hate, and to destroy one another, and via this online barrage, without reprisal.

In my vulnerable state the trolling monsters had invaded my personal space. My mind was clouded by fear. Most days the burden of carrying on was too heavy.

I know that hurt is part of life. I understand that. But I also know it's not something we should inflict on others. It's also not something to absorb submissively when it is cruelly directed our way. Not something we have to tolerate. My inner anguish put me in my self-imposed prison. Though I searched for joy and hope, my mind offered none.

Yet here, in what seemed an instant, I'd allowed invisible brutes to take away my joy. Panic attacks took over — 24/7.

SOCIAL MEDIA HAS FOREVER CHANGED OUR LIVES. Now we can engage with others from behind our keyboards. While so many positives exist about the digital revolution, it has also unleashed, or made obvious, the worst in society. Gossip and bullying were always part of the dark undercurrent of our society. Now, with anonymity, faceless beasts can spew hatred to complete strangers. Online trolls, it seems, thrive on the hurt they cause. They've lost the very spirit of our humanity.

While many times I'd tell myself to ignore the comments I was also ignoring that same advice from others to not check. I wanted to read and respond. It felt, when I read the messages, that I had leeches crawling on my skin, steering me towards the next and the next posts.

When the distributor in Cape Town alerted me to a post on their social media pages and advised me not to respond, I sat staring at the comments until anger rose and I wanted to scream at them to read my book and not focus on the word apartheid. Sometimes, when I'd taken a break from the continual checking, well-meaning friends would alert me to comments. Invariably my resolve would weaken and I'd read and fume. Sit fuming at the comments and think of retribution.

At home, as the weeks turned into months, my mental state declined. Pictures of my early life under oppression paralysed me. And I was crushed by thoughts of people reading my story and dismissing my pain.

When I wasn't checking for messages, I passed the time either in bed or sitting on our back deck or in bed. Chris managed to coax me out sometimes and we'd go for drives to the beach. I stared at the vast ocean and breathed in healing fresh air and exhaled my pent-up emotions. I felt safe, reassured in Chris's company and at times I could just sit with him and cry.

To allay my fears or merely distract me, he'd discuss home improvement projects and plans to redecorate my office. These projects, usually things that I'd relish, held no interest for me at all. I had been so deeply sucked in by self-loathing, that isolation was my comfort; something contrary to the essence of my spirit.

The sight of my book now repulsed me. It pained me to read the chapter about my little brother Owen's drowning. The words a potent reminder of that and other tragic events of my life. Here was my spirit in all its vulnerability. I had to find some way of making peace with it.

Since the launch we'd stopped accepting invitations from friends or going out to dinner. On the times I tried to venture out, I'd return home after a short while, defeated by anxiety and panic and helpless to fight it. I'd crawl into bed and listen to music.

Chris's shielding me was reassuring, but there were times it frustrated me, in a sense, suffocated me. I had trouble believing that my wings would work. That I could fly high into the sky where I was at my happiest.

As my spirited personality and independence floundered my resolve weakened. The only way through, I now thought, was with medical intervention.

THE ONE CHAPTER IN PARTICULAR that moved many readers was about Owen, and his drowning. It was also the part which aroused some of the most hurtful and inconsiderate comments. One reader wrote on my book page that she was truly moved by Owen's chapter but wanted to question why no one watched over him. Often, it's other's questions that awaken one's own.

At times, when the darkness engulfed me, I could smell the flowers surrounding Owen's body at his funeral. With it, came an immense sense of guilt. *Why could I not have saved him from drowning?*

I was older. I should have watched over him instead of splashing around in the dam with the other children. I would replay the vision of Owen walking towards us in the dam on that fateful day. He was so little; the water covered him in no time. *Why did I let him die?*

My longing also grew for my father, and my older brother, George. I reran our last conversation, on a visit to Cape Town, before he died over and over in my mind. He had the look on his face, the look that made me love him so much. He promised me he'd stop drinking, that he'd settle down with his partner, Helen, and continue to build a new life. I wanted to believe him, but I knew he was lying. He would never stop. We hugged, I cried and he cried and soon I flew back to Australia. Six months later, back in Cape Town, I looked at his body in a coffin. A few days earlier, I had listened to him taking his last breath over the phone.

When my oldest sister, Frances, died, there was a devastating rift in our family and it prevented me from fully grieving her death. All of us dealt with her death in our own way. I was consumed with guilt and hopelessness and replayed family memories. We were once eight. Now we are four. Pictures of them and our lives filled most waking moments; there was the city we'd left, countless difficult times. And of course, alongside, hundreds of happy ones.

And now, with Frances gone, my grief was boundless.

Back in Australia, the publisher encouraged me to engage with the media and public to promote the book, to increase sales. This was, after all, my just reward. But any event became increasingly challenging to prepare for and deliver. I agonised about it, but felt I had to cancel events and decline new bookings for a while.

At one local writer's festival, a few months earlier, a stranger had approached me after listening to my reading. His expression and tone of voice indicated that he was not there to congratulate me.

'What do you think about South Africa now?' he hissed.

'How did the country benefit from abolishing apartheid? What you're writing about is history. Why aren't you writing about what's happening today. Innocent white farmers and their families being murdered, you know! Those are the stories that should be told.'

I went to move and he moved in closer.

I looked straight at him. 'Don't dismiss my personal history,' I said.

'Your story is rubbish. It's ancient. People have moved on from that. What are you doing here, why aren't you back there if you agree with the current government? Have you seen the state of the country? That's what you all fought for, isn't it? Freedom. Go back, enjoy it. Let's just see how long you last.'

Usually I would have the courage, the strength to respond. Talk about the benefits of white privilege achieved at our disadvantage. But I had to get away. Shoving his arm away, I walked over to the snack table. I was shaking and disappointed that I couldn't defend myself. I escaped to the safety of our home.

In my bedroom, I lost myself browsing the internet, things uplifting. I read and read. The four walls, my bed and bedcover gave me the security I needed.

In this safe space, sobs racked my body until fear subsided and slowly, in the silence that followed drifted off to sleep. Until dreams, the kind I'd been plagued by all my life, shattered my peace.

CHAPTER THREE
HEALING, MY SEARCH

One of the principal aims of Shamanism is to dispel the false idea that you are not enough.

— Don Jose Ruiz

ON DAYS WHERE I COULD NOT GET OUT OF BED, my eyes would be glued to my screen researching traditional healing and holistic treatments. I felt strongly that allopathic, or Western, medicine alone wouldn't be enough to help me.

I had a deep longing to connect with my ancestors, to learn how they survived challenging times. Mum comes from a long line of strong women — she is one of thirteen sisters — and I wanted to draw on her family's strength and wisdom; dig myself out of this black hole.

In my search for natural therapies, I explored several healing modalities including holistic healing and spirituality; from kinesiology, to reiki, to acupuncture, herbal remedies and naturopathy. One night, desperate for something that would really resonate, I searched for a healer with psychic powers to predict my future or a medium who could help me make contact with my ancestors. I 'knew' that was what I needed; convinced that an evil spirit that had consumed my soul and I needed an exorcist.

Then, I came across shamanic healing and meditation. I read how traumatic events or setbacks can lead to our soul energies fragmenting, being depleted and leaving our spirit. These fragments could then get lost and spiritual healing could help retrieve them. I was intrigued. According to shamanic tradition, a regular clearance of negative energies and a restoration of energy balance would benefit anybody, everybody.

There are many reasons for our spirits to weaken or lose power; trauma may cause someone to lose some of their soul and personal power, affecting their ability to ward off illness. I felt my internal energies *were* depleted and wanted to reenergise myself.

One of the shaman's practices is to return a lost soul fragment. The more I researched the more comfortable I felt that this was going to be helpful.

A CALL FOR HELP FROM MY ANCESTORS, the powerful women in our family, would restore those parts of my soul, my spiritual force had been depleted. My forebears were women who worked as slaves, bore many children and tended to their families. I longed for their protection and healing from the powerless position I felt I was in. Negative thoughts overwhelmed me, daily. I'd allowed other people's messages to infiltrate my soul, batter my power.

The rituals from shamanic practitioners, would be able to elicit spiritual help and return me to my natural human fullness. So many of us already have daily rituals: we pray, meditate, sing, attend fellowship. When I read that shamanic practice is passed along in families, I felt a deeper connection to it. As someone who'd grown up with a strong religious faith, I believe in angels, in spirits and how deeply connected we are with our inner soul. I believe we have a purpose in our life journey and it's that connection that can carry us, successfully, through life. I also had a sense that I know, strongly, who I am. All I needed to know was within me. I may need help to uncover it, but I knew I could.

Shamans develop a personal style of cleansing to help ground people and deepen and strengthen their spiritual state. The shamanic rituals reminded me of those of specific people in our community; people who had spiritual gifts. One, in particular, a family friend, was a very wise strong man. Whenever he visited our home, his deeply spiritual words, healing hands and actions were always comforting. Moreover, he inspired us to believe in ourselves. At the time I was unaware of his healing gift. But he guided me in believing in the afterlife after my father died and I was struggling with the loss.

IN MY CURRENT STATE, spiritually depleted and mentally exhausted, my body felt under siege. In shamanic terms, I was subject to spiritual intrusions that had penetrated my body. The soul fractures had come from other human beings and through their greed for power; they'd gathered the power to alter the course of my soul's journey. Now I had allowed the memories of that life, childhood trauma and grief at the loss of my siblings to mull around and undermine my wellbeing.

Every day my search to find a local practitioner of these methods intensified. Shamans use drums and rattles to call on ancestors and spirits as a means to guide people through meditations, and into a shamanic state of consciousness.

Healers who work in the realm of the spirits reminded me so much of the wise elders in our communities who practised these type of healing methods. There was always someone in our communities who had healing powers. These treasured healers were revered and consulted on a myriad of medical issues. Their herbal remedies were the original natural medicines that generations have used successfully to treat ailments for thousands of years. Before modern medicine, natural remedies from herbs and common kitchen ingredients were often prepared to help the ailing patient. I remember talk of poultices moulded from bread and water, garden herbs, spices, vinegar and ground turmeric as the remedies for many ailments.

The rituals were something sacred and would be specific to my needs. With the right practitioner, I had the ability to reconnect my broken spirit.

Even with all that, I was somewhat fearful of losing myself in a shamanic trance. I kept on researching but hesitated for days before I tried one of the meditations I found online. My eagerness to heal myself had turned the caution into a growing willingness to trust the process.

I started with short meditations. I wanted to evolve, be able to tune into, listen to what my body was telling me. With that knowledge I could learn to drop my burdens and transform myself; to ground myself and be energetically cleansed. I could restore my balance.

These obsessive thoughts about retribution, and painful thoughts about the last moments of my siblings' earthly lives; and witnessing their deaths had embedded itself in my spirit. I struggled to let it go and felt depressed by the guilt and feelings of being unworthy of the privilege of a good life when they were robbed of theirs. *Why had their lives been cut so short?* They deserved to be in loving supportive relationships, working, enjoying their children and grandchildren. These emotions, finding peace and letting go, battled with each other across the boundaries of my mind weakening my ability to retain my spiritual power.

Convinced that shamanic practice would enable an energetic cleansing and increase my spiritual power and energy cemented the notion that this curse or spell could be removed. Also, retrieving the fragments of my soul would allow me to strengthen my immune system.

IN CAPE TOWN, the then Catholic Archbishop's parents were traditional healers. They learned the practice from Indigenous healers in South Africa. Their shop in our main street, was a symbol of traditional wisdom. Many potions, animal heads, claws and feathers adorned the shelves and walls. When my brother George started dating the Archbishop's sister, we learned more about their traditional practices.

Shamanic healers channel their spirit under the protection of a spirit animal and, through this altered state of consciousness, are able to access the spirit world, get guidance and perform healing. According to shamanic beliefs our spirit dwells in a reality different from the one we access in our 'normal' lives. When our bodies need healing so does our spirit.

Shamanic healing intrigued me even more when I learned about having a spirit animal. I needed the comfort of a spirit animal and researched more about shamanic meditation. It seemed, at that time, that all my waking moments were spent researching how a shamanic journey could pacify my heightened anxiety and panic disorder.

I'd practised my Catholic faith for most of my life: yet the prayers, Holy Mass and rituals no longer fulfilled my spiritual need. I needed a deeper connection that would link me more strongly with Spirit, with God, with the universe. My strong belief in an afterlife, in angels and the supernatural now, had begun to erase the fear of a shamanic journey. I'd become willing to embrace it with an openness and a deep longing to dwell in the realm of spirits and spirit animals for protection. That's where I felt most comfortable and secure.

Shamanic meditation — different from the meditation I was already practising — would allow me to work directly with my unconscious mind and observe my conscious thoughts.

My first 20-minute drum-assisted shamanic journey, performed in my loungeroom, was a journey into the unknown. Despite my usual fear of losing control of my surroundings, I had such a strong longing for calmness that it overcame the terror.

I lay on the floor, allowing my imagination to follow the guided meditation. Soon, I was drifting along a path filled with radiant light. On one long path I searched for a spirit animal in the beautiful surroundings. I was completely relaxed, and seeing myself in wonder-filled realms. Sounds of the forest filled my mind. In this sacred space, the sense of calm, filled my cells and brought me more peace than anything I'd tried before. By the end of my first journey, I knew I would practise this again and again.

Later, whenever I lacked concentration, I'd summon the comforting thought of a spirit animal and I'd refocus. I started longing for the comfort of my spirit animal in times of deep distress. This made me more determined to find a healer to help me, rather than keep going solo on this journey.

Years ago, I had seen the animated movie 'Mulan' which portrayed the role ancestors played in our lives. I was fascinated and longed for the wisdom and trust that ancestors could guide and intercede to help resolve our troubles. In another animated movie — 'Brother Bear' — the wise elder gives everyone a totem in the form of a spirit animal to protect them. That was the kind of protection I was drawn to before my sanity was overpowered.

WHILE I DISCUSSED MY FEELINGS about shamanism with Chris, he offered much support. But I was still reluctant to raise it with Sasha and Michelin. Or anyone else. I didn't want the label of 'hippie ritual' nor did I want to be splattered with too many questions, particularly from my son, Michelin — Mr Logic himself.

To protect myself from ridicule, I performed daily shamanic meditations in secret. I knew they'd scoff at this 'fantasy, bordering on ridiculous'. Yet, the shamanic meditation, prayers and walking were my comfort. These practices became my life line, a way to drift off to sleep and stop the bad dreams.

Soon I was swallowing different herbs and burning incense to ward off whatever spirit I believed possessed me. Ironically, whenever deep panic surfaced, I was comforted that there were spirits surrounding me; protecting me.

As the weeks passed, I obsessed about finding a local healer and scoured online sites for any leads. The ones I found were far away; I couldn't even get to them because driving was out of the question.

Slowly, then, my days had become unbearable and I believed that a guided deeply spiritual shamanic healing would be my answer. In the many hours I had behind the laptop, I persisted with the search. There had to be someone who would be able to help me.

CHAPTER FOUR
AN UNBURDENING BEGINS

Courage doesn't mean you don't get afraid.
Courage means you don't let fear stop you.

— BETHANY HAMILTON

IN LATE NOVEMBER 2018, after several weeks of meditation, I was able to venture outside onto the back deck and sit for a while lost in my thoughts. Still unable to write or venture outside the perimeter of our house, I thought more about my need for professional help. The birds chirping away, always close by kept my spirits up. I started believing that the birds could be my spirit animal. I became increasingly concerned about the festive season approaching and how I would cope with my growing isolation.

I felt calmer but my fears didn't disappear. Fear — always creeping in, crushing my spirit. When I felt desperately alone and frightened, I called Chris. Sometimes 000.

THE DECISION TO GET PROFESSIONAL HELP meant having to visit a new GP. God forbid he recommends medication. Our trusted GP of over 30 years, Dr Ismail Abdurahman had recently died and I missed him. Missed our spirited debates about life in South Africa, his wisdom, calmness and dry humour, and, not least, his dedication to his profession and patients. He had the knack of distracting me with stories about the past whenever I saw him.

So I had Dr Abdurahman's standards as my benchmark. The

new doctor ordered blood tests, particularly to check my thyroid. Then, offered a few suggestions to relieve my symptoms. First was a list of medications for me to consider. His recommendation for mood-altering medication to relieve my sleep disturbances was based on his diagnosis of generalised anxiety, panic, obsessive compulsive disorder and depression. Two pretty disturbing lists!

I refused to accept the diagnosis — especially from someone who hadn't really taken the time to get to know my condition deeply. I might have had the signs, body vibrations, hair loss, tired eyes and headaches lasting for days, but I was looking for some other diagnosis and treatment. I had been self-medicating, for months.

I'd been hitting on one 'solution' to another, one antihistamine to another, taking many natural remedies. But I wasn't willing to medicate to the degree he suggested. It was becoming absolutely clear that I needed a different type of professional practitioner to guide my healing.

NOT ONLY BECAUSE OF MY INTUITION about it, but also because the symptoms I went to the doctor with were not the only difficulties I was having. A year before my book launch, I'd been diagnosed with benign paroxysmal positional vertigo (BPPV), as the cause of balance issues whose symptoms included severe spinning, blurred vision, dizziness and poor balance. A young intern at our local hospital first mentioned that my spinning could be vertigo. I'd never heard of it so I researched the condition to find a specialist. I couldn't find any, neither did my GP recommend one. But during my research I did come across the Brain Hub, where a definite diagnosis of BPPV was made.

Several weeks after my first episode I consulted a chiropractor and neuro-vestibular rehabilitation practitioner, Dr Carlo Rinaudo, from the Brain Hub, the symptoms had abated somewhat. For a while, he was my lifeline. I had come across Carlo during my research into BPPV. He had a most impressive CV — researcher in vestibular neuro rehabilitation, lecturer and international speaker. The more I read about his work, the more I felt he could help me where other doctors could not.

At my first appointment, his test results showed my sense of balance as that of a much older person. My fear of falling during simple balance tests was exacerbated by my spatial disorientation.

Carlo was always on the other side of the phone or email to offer practical advice. I trusted him and made significant improvements with my balance complications under his care.

However, despite my BPPV symptoms lessening, the spinning now only happened if I slept in a certain position and, more often, nausea and disorientation followed. In July 2017, we were weeks out from travelling on a long-awaited trip to Italy to attend the golden jubilee celebrations of our close friend, Father Gerard Masters. Chris's excitement was tangible. The BPPV sent my anxiety levels through the roof and I had been ready to cancel, scared I'd land up in a hospital in Italy. But with Carlo's treatment program and reassurance my condition improved.

We remained committed to making the trip and, having decided to take along our granddaughters, Chelsea and Charlotte, I was determined to make it a memorable experience for everyone. Having the girls along gave me some comfort that, if anything happened, Chris would not be on his own.

Once in Rome, the reunion with Gerard, and all the activities planned and the excitement of the girls, kept my mood upbeat.

The trip to Italy had fallen in the middle of preparations for my sold-out annual charity ball, just one of the community events I used to produce. I tried to hide my work from Chris while we were on the trip, because he'd be concerned about my stress levels with a big event looming. But I couldn't. Some days, after a full and exhausting round of sightseeing in the searing heat, I'd spend hours online to ensure that everything was in place for the event, while Chris and the girls slept. Working to the point of exhaustion was how I controlled my anxiety. Many times, this pattern allowed me to fall into a deep sleep before nightmares would wake me.

IN SYDNEY, WHEN I'D FIRST ANNOUNCED that The Rockets, a popular group from South Africa, was the headline band for the charity ball, tickets sold out in no time. The tight schedule required impeccable planning, leaving no room for flight delays or lost equipment or any complication. As always, back in control, my brain kicked into gear, a few notches higher than usual.

Towards the end of our visit to Italy, after a visit to Pompeii and Naples, I suffered an episode of BPPV, forcing me to rest for the last two days before our long flight home. Carlo had booked me straight back into treatment soon after we landed.

Once home, despite my ongoing BPPV, I was back running the show and preparing for the big night. The charity ball, was a popular event on my calendar; my pride and joy. The Rockets, a renowned band of my youth, had arrived and were raring to entertain the large crowd in Sydney and at a side show in Melbourne the night before. The theme, a Spring Ball, was highly anticipated.

On the night, I greeted everyone with my smile firmly in place. Months of negotiation, the stringent visa process, union approval, flights, accommodation, travel, promotion, transport, production and ticket sales all fell on me. Liaison between venue production staff and the band (tricky at the best of times) left me to negotiate and calm things during technical set up. But at showtime they turned into professional mode. At the band and technical staff turned into professional mode.

Sasha, my ultimate wing person on staff, with Chris, Chelsea, Charlotte, Michelin and Lisa, was there to pick up the slack or satisfy my demands without a murmur. Of course, only out of earshot! Showbusiness ran through my veins, stemming from a backyard dream on the Cape Flats for the ten-year-old me.

That's where I started dreaming of holding concerts. I'd round up the neighbourhood children during school holidays and produce my own plays to stage in our backyard. Now, I produced concerts on real stages!

Regardless of my meticulous planning I catastrophised. Only when I heard the sound of the applause from the adoring crowd could I retreat to my safe place. But the earlier, and repeated anxiety had exhausted me. The only way to alleviate it was to duck backstage to sit isolated from the crowd. And even there, I was wracked with self-criticism. *Why can't I just be normal, relax and relish in the success of the night?*

This was my vicious cycle. Outwardly coping; inwardly falling apart. Diligent preparation; continual self doubt. A soul-destroying condition.

When BPPV first struck, affecting my balance, I processed that as a sign I was not worthy of these opportunities. Thought my working life was over.

DESPITE REHABILITATION AT THE BRAIN HUB where Carlo and the team worked diligently to improve my symptoms, my brain struggled to cope with the spatial confusion. Fears of falling had skyrocketed and my anxiety levels increased. And Carlo was always there, giving me the tools to manage my condition should it flare up unexpectedly.

'How long will BPPV last?' I asked. 'Can it be cured?'

'These conditions can last for seconds or days. In some instances, though, they persist,' he said. Oh, I thought. That's for life.

At the same time, I tried to be conscious that my ailments were not life-threatening. When, a few years earlier, after being diagnosed with a debilitating eye condition, the gifted, late Dr Evan Soicher, gently advised me my brain would start ignoring these round floating clouds. I was sceptical. Evan taught me coping mechanisms should the condition flare up unexpectedly.

Over subsequent years I had to admit he was right about my brain function! Now, I told myself, I could hope the same thing would happen with BPPV.

Common yet, sometimes more debilitating, effects of many chronic vestibular conditions are symptoms of anxiety, fear and depression. Recent medical science draws a link between the vestibular system to parts of the brain regulating emotions, memory, cognitive, mood, social interaction and attention.

There's a strong relationship between our vestibular system and our spatial orientation and navigation. And, if someone has a prior history of anxiety, depression and hypervigilance, as well as migraines or concussions, there's a higher likelihood of these associated symptoms or effects.

THE WHOLE 'PACKAGE' MEANT that at times, I'd frantically scan my body for signs of illness so I could stay in bed. Headaches equalled tumours; a cold equalled pneumonia and lung collapse. A racing pulse could mean a heart attack. These thoughts played havoc with my sanity. At times, I'd have to get off a train before my stop and sit down and wait for the panic to pass. Sometimes I'd leave the dinner table and head to the nearest bathroom to count tiles.

Seeking help to overcome my vestibular disorder, was not plain sailing. However, from the first day I stepped into the Brain Hub, Carlo gained my confidence. For the first time I felt heard and understood. The clinic's equipment, its targeted and integrative therapies and their exercises to recalibrate the whole system, helped to address my vestibular 'mismatch'.

Despite the return of my BPPV symptoms, I felt confident that healing was in progress because I was under Carlo's care. My pathway to coping and healing was to be found not only through science but also through continuous reassurance and guidance from a supportive team and family support. This was the kind of support I wanted. It was the support I needed.

CHAPTER FIVE
HOW MUCH LONGER?

*I can't go back to yesterday
because I was a different person then.*

— LEWIS CARROLL

DESPITE ALL MY GP'S TESTS and checks, there was no specific diagnosis and he attributed everything to stress and depression.

To raise my spirits, I wanted to get back to doing what I loved — creating, writing, working, talking and, most important, laughing. My now continuing digestive issues needed attention; he wanted to prescribe more medication. When my results were normal, in fact I had excellent blood results, he confirmed his earlier diagnosis that my mental health was in need of addressing.

His suggestions for treatment of my mental state included a list of medications. I was horrified; I read worrying reviews of the suggested drugs with one worse than the other. He selected one recommendation from the list and suggested I research it and then come back for a prescription.

How can this be my life? A life of medication and a zombie-like state. What if I missed out on everything I'd worked so hard to achieve, or got hooked?

For days I wept in self-pity. This was not what I had envisioned for my life. I'd tried keeping all the things inside but now the pain has become harder to ignore. I went back to the doctor. Surely there was another solution? Another way to get back to enjoying my life again.

'Well, then I recommend cognitive behavioural therapy. Here's a list of local psychologists,' he said handing over a full page. 'Let me know which one you'd like to go to.'

GOOGLE, MY GO-TO 'EXPERT' provided a lot of information about his suggested therapists. I focused on their social media pages, websites and explanations of their therapy and started the elimination process.

Then, the Tibetan monk perched on a rock overlooking a valley caught my attention. It was the opening page of clinical psychologist Dr Geoff Lyons' website. He'd listed his extensive areas of expertise including his spiritual and holistic mental health care approach. On the top of his list of conditions he treated: anxiety and panic disorders.

I dived into researching everything about him — where he'd studied, his publications, his descriptions of his approach. And I came on his doctoral thesis: *Spirituality, forgiveness and purpose in life in faith-based substance abuse treatment programs*. What rang the loud bell was that this is an issue that affected our family and was pertinent to the community in which I grew up. In many of the papers he'd published, his words reflected my struggles.

Mostly, though, the principles of the practice — spiritual and holistic clinical treatment — piqued my interest. Clearly, this would be a drug-free healing practice and could be the place to ease my crippling fears. I needed a practitioner who would understand, even share, my interest in ancient wisdom, ancestors, spirits and angels. Someone from whom there'd be no ridicule or judgement. Someone who wouldn't see me as a crazy, hallucinating human (and have the straitjacket ready).

On the rare occasions I'd tried to talk about my pain with friends and family, their first impulse was to jump in with advice. Well meaning, no doubt. And usually full of platitudes about how to let the pain go and flow and any number of rather banal pieces of advice. Worse, some would hijack the conversation to explain their (invariably more serious) problems. I'd invariably withdraw deeper, and switch off or spend the entire time listening.

Gone were dinner parties and catching up with friends. Even our parish was now a 'no-go' area. Despite it being a spacious church, I felt claustrophobic as soon as I sat down in a pew. So my silent prayers were said in the comfort of my bedroom. On occasion, I'd pray aloud (to wake the spirits).

While I talked to Mum on the phone regularly, I hadn't visited her for a few months. I missed visiting my brother Andy, who was in rehabilitation following spinal surgery. I felt deep guilt about not being there for Andy when he needed me. I seldom saw my younger sister, Maureen, who'd moved interstate. There were regular phone calls but nothing to replace seeing and talking and laughing face-to-face. I needed the physical support from a sibling or someone I could pour my heart out to and then laugh about the ridiculousness of my fears.

I missed my late sister, Frances, more and more. She'd understand my feelings about Owen. We had sat for hours and talked about that fateful day and our memories of his short life. I could discuss our childhood, moan about how poor we were, rail against apartheid's general and specific ugliness. Only she understood the significance of the things we dreamed about as children, real things like, for her, a cookie jar filled to the brim. For me, an overflowing fruit bowl. As adults we always made sure those symbols of abundance, were made real in our homes.

WITH MY DAILY ROUTINE IN DISARRAY and my concentration at almost its lowest point, I had stopped writing anything other than a few hundred words whenever I could. The only reading I did was for a cure for my ailments.

I wanted a tranquil mind. And the image of the monk and the valley, oozed tranquillity. The longer I stared at the image, the more convinced I was that I could find healing there. The serenity of the valley held promise of restoring calm and comforting my aching spirit.

I booked an appointment.

Then started counting the days till it was time to meet the monk (well, his friend, at least). I longed to speak my truth, and without fear of correction, or disapproval or judgement or, at the worst, false comfort. I needed empathy and kindness before my healing could begin.

MY FIRST VISIT TO GEOFF'S OFFICE could not have prepared me for the emotional healing journey that lay ahead. Sutherland Shire bushland, a 15-minute drive from home, seemed the perfect setting. Chris accompanied me because I was unable to drive my car, and hadn't slept well for days.

I entered the practice. A strange, eerie stillness hung over the semi-lit space and the large room looked as if it was used for yoga or meditation. In the centre of the large room, a blanket was spread out on the floor. A brass bowl was placed in the middle of the blanket between pillows. A faint scent of incense filled the air. *Isn't this illegal? Where are the smoke detectors? Do they offer their clients weed?*

Then, the familiar feelings, my stomach churning and the muscle tremors jolted me back to reality. I could feel it — fear, rising. *Is this the wrong place?* I should have asked more questions when I made the appointment. *What method will he use? Will I go into a trance during therapy?*

While I was optimistic this could be the start of my road to recovery, I didn't have the foggiest idea what I would say. My mind was already in overdrive. *This is a mistake. Was there still time to get out?*

But the door to a room in the far corner had opened and I caught a glimpse of a smiling, friendly man walking towards me.

'I'm Geoff Lyons,' he said. 'And you are Beryl Segers, right?'

He looked too young. What would he know about my life and troubles?

He handed me a clipboard with papers and a pen, looked directly at me, locking his eyes to mine while he talked. *Can he hear how wildly my heart is beating and how I am willing myself to stay calm?*

To hide my fear, I gripped the pen, twisting it to steady my trembling hands. I smiled back at him but I was desperate to focus elsewhere. *He is so white. His eyes are too blue.* During my research, I had been so engrossed with what he offered that I paid little attention to his picture. Now he looked so much younger than the image on his social media pages. In my fragile state, blond hair and blue eyes were reminders of privilege.

This wouldn't do. I needed to talk to someone who'd understand my memories of oppression, my resentment about racial inequality, my search for a connection to my ancestors and the impact all my memories had on my psyche. He didn't fit that mould. Would he be someone who'd say, 'That's something your ancestors are to blame for?'

'Don't think too much about the answers,' he said. 'Just put down what comes to mind, I'll come back out shortly.'

Who is he talking to? He obviously doesn't know who he is dealing with? My brain will analyse every inch of these forms before I complete them. These questions will be reanalysed, deconstructed and then I'll question their validity. His voice faded into the background as I scanned the questionnaire.

The header on one form scared me. He wanted to measure my anxiety and depression. I started ticking the boxes, then changed my mind a few times. 'How many times have you felt hopeless this week?' *How do I answer that?* If I say every day, will he recommend I go to a mental health institution where they'll keep me in a drug-induced state? *What do I say? Once? Yes, OK, I'll say once.*

My mind drifted to how many times I *had* felt hopeless. Every single day. Nightmares shattered my sleep: there was drowning, a car crash, a flood, wind storms, falling off a mountain, chasing by monsters, or a hot air balloon plummeting to the ground.

Can I mention the days I couldn't get into my car to drive onto the street? Or count how many times I managed to pull it out of the driveway only to drive straight back in again?

My life felt truly hopeless in the middle of the night, with everyone else soundly asleep, when I wandered around the house. That's when. *How can I tell some stranger that my dreams keep me awake every night?*

But I am diligent. So I kept ticking the boxes to sound like a pretty reasonable person. *Everything is going to be fine. I'm in the right place to get help.* At the bottom of the personal information, my heart skipped a beat. There were boxes to tick offering alternate healing modalities. Without hesitation I ticked *Yes* to all the boxes about energy and spiritual healing.

'Come this way to my room,' he said, still smiling, pointing in the direction of an open door.

I, however, would have preferred to sit on the floor in the big open space, absorb the aroma of the incense and just talk about life, magic, evolution and stuff.

Inside the small room, he gestured for me to sit on a beige coloured two-seater couch. He settled into a blue chair across from me. If he'd asked me how I was feeling, I'd have said, fearful and claustrophobic. A small candle flickered on the side table and I was ready to collapse on the small couch. Ah, the pillow. If only I could rest my head on it and drift off to sleep. I scanned the room for any sinister potions on the shelves. None.

A rolled-up yoga mat was propped against the wall, and a desk and bookshelves filled two walls. A painting, a small boat on a lake, caught my eye. I perused the book collection while he rattled off some formalities. My lifelong love affair with books carried me through many dark days.

Where am I supposed to stretch out? In the movies, people

stretched out on the couch in therapy rooms. But this couch was too small. *If only I could shut my eyes just for a few moments.*

Avoiding his piercing gaze, my eyes continued to scan the books on the shelf while he continued with what seemed like a prepared set of rules. I didn't pay much attention to what he was saying until he made reference to contact arrangements.

'We don't know each other outside this therapy room,' he said. That'll only be awkward for both of us.'

What? Awkward? I always stopped to talk to my GP whenever I met him outside in public. *What kind of rule is this?* So, I have to pour out my deepest feelings to someone who won't acknowledge me outside of this room.

I DIDN'T REALISE, at the time, the importance of that statement. Divulging deeply personal information to someone comes with a vulnerability so deep that a sense of trust and security is paramount to a therapeutic relationship.

While he talked, my eyes wandered back to the books, and one popped out *Post Traumatic Stress Disorder (PTSD)*. The title gave me shivers. *Is this what's wrong with me?*

Such serious topics among the yoga and spiritual books. I know he'll soon ask me why I am here. *Where do I start? How can I bare my soul? What would he know about my complex history? This is a mistake.* My mind raced until I spotted a brass bowl on the shelf. I had seen one like this before, in a yoga studio.

I had no idea how to broach the reason I'd come to see him. It sounded ridiculous, in that moment, to talk about the impact apartheid had on me. I've lived outside South Africa for over 30 years. *Why now and why such a deep effect? Why am I so consumed by memories from my childhood?*

My first instinct was to excuse myself, go to the bathroom, count tiles, splash water on my face and return a while later. But somehow, transfixed by his gentle gaze and relaxed posture, I managed to remain in my seat, though I was clutching the pillow next to me.

You are not crazy. You are not crazy.

I wanted to tell him that I wouldn't just listen to his words, but would pick up on his tone, his gestures, and facial expressions. I interpret silences and will be able to hear the words in the gaps of his sentences. But I kept that to myself for fear of being classified a weirdo.

This silence, I must break the silence. I wonder if he can hear my heart pounding in my throat?

'Tell me a bit about yourself,' he said. 'Where do you live? Are you working?'

Working? That's easy.

'I'm an author,' I heard the words tumble out.

'Really? What do you write?' he asked and seemed genuinely interested.

'I've been a writer since childhood, but earlier this year I published a family memoir about growing up in South Africa under apartheid,' I said.

'Congratulations, that's quite an achievement.' He smiled with such warmth that it made me smile.

'Every person has a story to tell,' I said.

'I'm sure that's true,' he said. 'But not everyone has the gift of writing their stories.'

In that one moment, something in me calmed. The room had a warmth and cosiness about it and my mind settled. Here was an ear to listen to my journey of self-discovery and unburdening. I was now determined to work hard here; work at this opportunity to bring tranquillity to my mind.

LITTLE DID I KNOW the pain and tears that would be part of this healing. The fight against my anxiety and crippling panic attacks was fraught with self-sabotage. Anxiety was like an addictive drug, a feeling that overpowered me, I needed more than positive thoughts and breathing to get me through an episode. At times, in my isolation, anxiety was my only friend.

Throughout the session I pushed down on the pillow to stop the trembling in my legs. Any reluctance to reveal my fears would not have been new to him. Guarded and on high alert, I answered his probing questions about my life. Geoff's easy and relaxed manner even had me smiling a few times. His eyes remained fixed on mine with such gentleness that I felt less vulnerable.

Occasionally he'd jot something on his notepad on the small table next to him. Whenever he wrote anything, I tried to follow his writing to decipher the notes. I kept my guard raised somewhat; the intense fear of landing up in a mental institution was uppermost in my mind.

We talked about my family and the challenges of three generations living together. As a father of three young girls, he empathised, with Chris's frustration, at times, of being surrounded by five hormonal females of differing ages — one of whom was a female puppy, Marley.

I wanted to tell him about my life before all this happened, not this messed up woman sitting across from him. *Could I dial a friend and let them tell him who I am? Or show him my awards or get a reference from those who know me.* This is not the person I wanted him to know. I was ashamed of being so weak and powerless, and vulnerable that I had landed in therapy. I am a victor not a victim. I have the track record.

In the past year, I had gone from someone who walked in their power to a crumbling, fearful person who now recoiled when approached. During the past year my mental decline was rapid as years of hidden pain unravelled. When my confidence was at its lowest and I was barely able to function, I tried to push on. I didn't succeed. I was no longer comfortable to look people in the eye, often taking the long way around when I spotted a familiar face. Bright lights, open spaces, traffic and loud noises unsettled me.

I was stuck in the past. The life I'd walked away from and tried to erase was now forefront, daily. It was clear to me and my family, now, that urgent intervention was needed. I needed support from a professional who wouldn't tell me to cheer up, or force me to snap out of whatever, or offer instructions on how to move on with life now that I'd published my book.

Strategies. I needed strategies to deal with my heightened fear and to confront my anger and resentment towards our oppressors. I needed to stop feeling ashamed of my mental health crisis.

Very few people knew about the bouts of anxiety and panic I've suffered over the years. I'd become a master at hiding my pain. There were many times I had to get off trains on my way to work to settle myself, before carrying on to my destination. Many times, of frantic escapes to bathrooms to unleash my pain before returning to my desk or rejoin a dinner party. I've sat on many bathroom floors and counted endless tiles until my fears subsided.

No one knew that. Everyone knew me as happy and smiling. A smile always in place.

Now, the reminders of my deprived life had resurfaced. The plague of pain spread through my cells. It felt as if a burning rash was spreading, reminding me that my skin was inferior. I'd thought those parts of my life were long buried. Yet underneath a successful exterior lurked grinding self-doubt.

Since arriving in Australia, I had built a life equal to others. I'd grabbed every opportunity, was unstoppable at the best of times, and reached heights in my chosen field that many in my circle dreamed about.

And now, it was me, looking around, consumed with envy at how others looked so relaxed, while I had to make a concerted effort to concentrate on what people were saying. The self-loathing surfaced at the oddest times; I believed no one else was having such a hard time dealing with their emotions. *Am I really crazy?* Maybe one of my ancestors was some crazy woman whose spirit had invaded my psyche. I wished there was some way to know when this would pass.

'I've been unwell but the doctor cannot find anything really wrong with me,' I said. 'I feel as if they are missing something.'

'How long have you been feeling unsettled?' he asked.

'Several months now,' I answered. 'My GP puts everything down to anxiety and depression and wants me to use medication, but I am reluctant. I want to explore alternate therapies. I don't know if I *am* depressed.'

He nodded. *How do I start telling him what is bothering me?* This weight is resting so heavily on my shoulders. Having to discuss triggers of my anxiety and panic disorder was challenging. It had become easier, for me, to suffer in silence. Yet that left others ill-equipped to know how to help me when I was in that dark place. Tears were forming. *Don't cry!*

'Tell me about your book,' I heard him say.

He looked directly at me as if to connect with my soul. I averted his gaze, and my tear-filled eyes wandered over to the bookshelf. At this very moment, going into details of my book was hard.

'Why the sadness?' he said gently.

'I'll bring you a copy of my book,' I said quickly to change the subject. 'You can read it when you have time.'

WHEN THE HOUR HAD PASSED, I was relieved but more surprised I'd managed to relax and talk about my family and mention the book. I had so much to share about my fears, the horrible things being said to me and my angst about my memories. At the end of the session he drew a diagram showing how medication worked in helping the brain to adjust. I looked on, incredulous, when he showed me how medication could stem the flow of activity to my brain and block out anxious thoughts.

'I'll book you in for next week?' he offered.

What struck me the most was that he looked genuinely interested in my wellbeing as he wished me well for the week. This was not just a practitioner talking to me about clinical strategies but someone who presented a deep empathy and sensitivity. Slowly I felt a relief, even while being conscious this was going to be no miracle cure, but the first step towards getting help. Even my sitting in his room, unburdening my fears was, in itself, a major achievement.

At home I resumed what had become my regular activities — meditation or solitude in my bedroom. And each new morning, despite that, I woke with tired eyes and sapped energy.

Chris, Sasha and Michelin eagerly awaited my news about what had happened. But I had very little information for them. I had no idea whether this would be successful or not.

CHAPTER SIX
THE HEALER

The secret of change is to focus all of your energy, not on fighting the old, but on building the new.
— Socrates

GEOFF'S PSYCHOLOGY AND HEALING practice was his dream. He studied psychology at university and it was there that he was inspired to create a space where he could spend his time helping people with mental health struggles. At the core of his approach was the scientific study of the human mind and its functions.

Early on in his studies, he felt a pull towards merging his strong basis in psychology training with his true passion — his understanding of, and learning about, spirituality. Together, these two understandings offered the breadth and depth that Geoff felt would offer a more holistic approach to healing. The more he worked and studied, the more he explored a wealth of modalities which would benefit his clients.

GEOFF LYONS PHD WAS BORN in the rural city of Griffith, in the Murrumbidgee Irrigation Area in south central New South Wales. His family relocated to Port Macquarie, before he was three, and it was in this coastal town on the mid-north coast that he spent his formative years into adulthood.

When Geoff was around nine his parents' marriage broke down and his father relocated to Queensland. While his father maintained contact with the family, the physical distance left

Geoff somewhat devoid of a male role model.

Geoff's mother, a teacher, was diagnosed with cancer, the first time, shortly before the marriage separation, and then again when Geoff was around twelve and entering high school. Her ill health meant she wasn't able to work.

As is often the case with divorce and serious illness, the family of four — Geoff, his mother, a younger sister, and older brother — were in reduced economic circumstances. There was little contact with extended family, which resulted in feelings of isolation and more hardship.

While Geoff is, today, a passionate professional, it wasn't obvious from his early school years that this would be the case. He never imagined pursuing a tertiary education nor were such things discussed at home. Because of his impoverished background Geoff never dared to think there was a way for him to do this, nor did he ever really want such a thing. He assumed a university education was something for the other kids who could afford it, not for him.

IN FACT, AS A YOUNG BOY Geoff wanted nothing more than a life of adventure. For him, being a hero, a warrior would mean something. He was a kind boy, introverted and yet his mischievous nature would sometimes emerge. Rules, from school, from his family, all felt like limitations. The way he felt most accommodated was when people left him to his own devices. Where he could be truly himself and do what he wished.

Without judgement. He longed for something exciting and purposeful to do with his life; something that would explain why he existed. To him understanding what life was really for, seemed like an obvious question, yet he didn't see this enquiry reflected in the broader community. Australian culture seemed obsessed with sport, politics and celebrities— things he thought were not worth spending too much time on. By the time he turned 14 he'd become disillusioned. He thought the real world/

mainstream world was far too dull and painful. And, that everyone he knew took things he found trivial, all too seriously. His dream then? For a tribal world, where global ideas mattered. To get away from things; become a hermit. Though he knew that was impossible. He was trapped.

Lacking motivation, discipline or a home environment conducive to study, Geoff would half-heartedly attempt his homework, more focused on whatever was playing on the family television than the textbook lying in front of him. He was consumed by sci-fi films and fantasies. This ability to get lost in a dream world carried him through his teenage years. He found his heroes in sci-fi movies, comic books and fantasy novels. In fact, some of these mystical beings — Luke Skywalker for one — became the role models he never had in real life.

GEOFF, UNLIKE MANY OF THIS SCHOOL FRIENDS who came from more affluent backgrounds, had to find part-time work on weekends to supplement the family income. While his friends had the freedom to socialise, even to study, Geoff was at his retail job.

He liked working hard and earning money. But he disliked the fact that it distanced him even more from his friends. Geoff's ability to work and earn money from such a young age also cemented his ambivalence towards education. His young mind had quite a limited perspective: he was already making money so why keep studying.

After completing high school however Geoff began to drift from one retail job to another, while he watched many of his friends go to university. It was obvious that he lacked direction and was never fully satisfied with his achievements.

Suddenly the sense of inferiority which had been a quiet whisper grew loud. But his mother was very supportive and reassuring. She urged him to have patience. She tried to instil in him the confidence she had that he'd find his way. It brought as much dread as it did solace though because he had no idea where to even start or if he ever would find it.

WHEN HE TURNED 21, and after much deliberation about leaving his family, Geoff moved to Sydney to find work. He found various labouring jobs, mostly laying carpet and roofing and then, he made a complete change and joined the army.

It meant a place where he could learn a trade, get a career and some much-needed stability and direction. The army, however, had other plans. They rejected this career path and suggested he was better suited to being an officer.

For a young man who thought he had no future other than, perhaps, being a mechanic, it was both flattering and validating to get the recognition that he had what it took to be an Army Officer. He knew it was a gamble. But it was also an opportunity to have a meaningful role.

The fact that his father was deeply proud at the idea of his son being an officer, helped Geoff's decision. So he pushed aside his nagging thought, his intuition, that he wasn't truly suited to an officer role and enlisted. Within a few months, he began his training at the Royal Military College, Duntroon.

IT WASN'T LONG BEFORE HIS FEARS became reality and he found the army culture was also unsuited to his gentle nature. Initially things went well and he was recognised as a promising cadet. He had good friends too, but they were more the gentle and intellectually-inclined officer cadets.

Then, one-by-one these friends left the college. Some because they were disenchanted with the harshness of army culture, others were injured or ill, another few, to go to university. Geoff stayed for 12 months. But when he was unrelentingly disillusioned with army culture and realised he was too sensitive to make himself fit in, he decided to leave. He was left however with a pervasive sense of failure, the beginnings of a depression, and a question of what his next steps could possibly be.

One thing he desperately missed from his time in the military was time spent in nature, time in the outdoors. Some of his training meant sleeping under the stars or hours hiking through fields, mountains and bushland. This inspired him, felt real to him and he understood this was, now, one of his passions. In the weeks and months after he left Duntroon, he'd go for long walks in the local bushland of Sydney's Sutherland Shire. He spent many hours sitting in stillness, absorbed by the energy of the earth and trees around him. He thought of a career as a park ranger, and decided, that he'd go to university as a mature-age student to study. A park ranger, after all, protected nature and could be a good fit for a young warrior.

HE BEGAN A DEGREE in Environmental Science at the University of Wollongong, however, in his first semester something unexpected happened to his career plans. Geoff had begun practising meditation as a means of addressing his lingering sense of failure.

Meditation was not unfamiliar to him. He'd been enrolled, at age ten, in a local martial arts school where he started learning Hapkido, a highly eclectic Korean martial art. It is a form of self-defence; he learnt joint locks, grappling and throwing techniques, and began to gain the sense of adventure his comic books and sci-fi movies were filled with.

His first instructor, a Chinese medicine practitioner, soon became one of Geoff's role models. This man instilled in his students a holistic approach to the martial arts, occasionally sharing stories of his acupuncture work and the existence of chi — an energy system that exists throughout the body.

For a young boy with a strong pull to fantasy, this was a perfect fit. Geoff continued practising hapkido and other martial arts on and off into his early 30s, and it was through this that he grew more interested in the meditation his instructors had taught and the resulting calmness during and after the practice that his instructors had taught

IT WAS ONLY WHEN HE LEFT the military, however, that Geoff's journey into the world of meditation truly began. His significant insight, at that time, was that his problems were, predominantly, of his own making. He alone was responsible for his life, his successes but also, his failures.

He had never fully applied himself to anything — a realisation that lit a fire in his belly and was stoked by his new meditation practice.

Multiple times a day he'd meditate, sitting in the half-lotus posture. Although he had been introduced to meditation in his hapkido classes these practices were always brief and happened irregularly. So, he was relatively self-taught. Later, having completed a formal yoga teacher training, he refined his techniques. The meditation practice was amplifying his spiritual interests. It was also enhancing his qualities of sensitivity and his enquiring mind. He could feel himself growing more compassionate, intuitive, motivated and patient. The meditation and yoga practices opened up new and deeper connections to his inner world. He became more skilled at observing his thoughts as well as finding a deeper sense of who he really was.

As he became more interested in the ideas of consciousness, of the mind he wondered if he could learn more about meditation through psychology. He began to toy with the idea of studying psychology. He also thought there might be scope to one day help young men like himself. There was, though, a roadblock.

He was still enrolled in Environmental Science and the last thing he wanted was to add a non-completed degree to his list of failures. So, with caution, he enrolled in some first-year psychology subjects, found them satisfying and completed them successfully. It gave him the confidence to transfer his studies formally to psychology.

AT THE SAME TIME as doing his undergraduate psychology degree, he completed a diploma in yoga and became a yoga teacher. It was rewarding but also a challenge to fit one more thing into an already full life.

More challenging still, his immersion in yogic literature and practices was enticing him with familiar adolescent fantasies of leaving mainstream society and becoming a monk. These were serious thoughts that fitted seamlessly with his introverted disposition and were amplified by the changes he was experiencing in his own consciousness. For many years he forced himself to stay with his psychology studies; his intuition was telling him this was an important part of his journey.

The pull towards a monastic life became even more problematic in his mid-20s when he met and started dating a young girl who would one day become his wife. This was a very hard period of his life where he felt absolutely conflicted by two competing demands: to be away from society and completely devoted to his spirituality or be with the woman he loved and, with that, be part of a family.

An added factor was his sense — very strong intuition — that this woman would be the mother to his children. After several years of dating he realised that his love for this girl was too strong. Besides leaving society to become a monk would be simply running away, and that more spiritual development, purpose and satisfaction would ultimately be achieved through the harder path —committing to marriage and fatherhood. Eventually, he was married and became father to three beautiful girls. To this day Geoff has a great deal of sympathy for young people struggling with the transition into marriage and parenthood.

WHEN PRACTISING HIS YOGA POSTURES, Geoff would often experience deep relaxation. During his meditations he occasionally felt himself floating outside his body or experienced an expansion of consciousness that was hard to put in words.

These things convinced him that there was a transcendental element to human development that his psychology textbooks, with all their talk of statistics and experimental design, were simply not addressing. How could psychology, he asked himself, which was historically defined as the study of the soul, relegate spirituality to a fringe interest? How can psychology professors with years of clinical experience focus only on the objective analysis of thoughts and behaviours without any mention of the energies of the body, or meditation, or a deeper, more transcendental purpose in life? Geoff felt he achieved more personal development through a diploma of yoga than a degree in psychology. He was disappointed with the hours of study spent on academic topics like vision and perception, memory and learning and the acquisition of language and thinking processes. He longed for a class on meditation or the psychology of religion and spirituality. They never came.

PSYCHOLOGY HAS DEVELOPED a great deal in the last decades and is now much more holistic, such that the use of a range of meditation practices has become a mainstream field of study. 'Energy psychology' is a legitimate topic of investigation, psychology professors routinely run to yoga classes in their spare time, and the exploration of values and their contribution to wellness is a core topic that psychologists pay attention to.

But at the time Geoff was studying, topics like these were not on the curriculum and, perhaps, not even on the agenda of his fellow professionals.

Geoff's concerns followed him throughout his studies and into his professional career. What began as a confusion, became a frustration and eventually, consolidated his determination to change the way he would work in the psychological field. He was committed to a holistic approach and the desire to explore a broader holistic clinical philosophy would become the driver, throughout his career. Like a bird with two wings — psychology and spirituality — Geoff found his path.

IT WAS IN THE UNIVERSITY LIBRARY, where he visualised starting his own practice. Psychology could offer him a pathway into this career yet his approach to serving others would need to be a merger; a true and successful blend of a broad skill set; more than that offered by traditional psychology.

The opportunity to complete a doctorate, through a scholarship from the University of Wollongong, presented a crucial step in Geoff's journey. His PhD thesis explored the role of spirituality in the recovery from substance abuse of clients attending Salvation Army drug and alcohol rehabilitation centres. He had the chance to integrate scientific psychology with Christian theology and it rekindled his enthusiasm for Christian mysticism which he'd studied years earlier during his yoga training.

It was not an easy integration. He struggled to blend Christian doctrines with yogic literature and he was in the throes of spiritual turmoil for many years. The Church had told him yoga and meditation were dangerous practices; his heart, and own mystical experiences, told him they were a pathway to truth. It was, as he says, a spiritual dissonance that lasted for many years. Eventually, he found a balance between the two perspectives and, in the process, gained a deep empathy for those experiencing spiritual crises.

AFTER COMPLETING HIS PhD, Geoff worked in various hospitals and, through his clinical practice, was exposed to a broad spectrum of techniques. His first role as a clinical psychologist was in a facility for young women with eating disorders.

Empathic and kind, Geoff empathised with the young people distressed by such a debilitating mental condition. Though he wasn't always comfortable as a male in a female-dominated clinical population, he was very good at the role and found it greatly rewarding. Taking patients to meals, leading group therapy and supporting their wellbeing on the hospital ward came easily to Geoff, who appeared relaxed despite a measure of vigilance always present. It was not uncommon for the patients to experience anxiety attacks seemingly from nowhere. In a flash, Geoff, as psychologist, would be on deck to calm and help them.

AFTER HIS WORK IN EATING DISORDERS Geoff moved onto an area he was deeply interested in — palliative care. He was able to share his spiritual awareness during his work in palliative care wards providing end-of-life therapy to terminally ill patients. It is there he felt a true calling.

It was not a struggle talking with patients about their life-limiting illnesses, fears of death and the afterlife. Instead, he felt a real purpose in these dialogues. He felt at ease helping patients and their families navigate this stage of life and considered it a great honour.

When he was deciding to conduct more research on spirituality and mental health, he had to make one of the hardest decisions of his career. It would mean leaving oncology and palliative care to pursue academic opportunities.

In 2013, around the time he left palliative care, Geoff opened his own practice — both as a means of supplementing the family income but also a way to start attracting and working with more spiritually-minded clientele. He was on his way to fulfilling the destiny he had imagined so many years earlier. It did not come without difficulty.

Geoff was an academic during the day, teaching psychology students how to assess personality, measure intelligence, conduct therapy, design experiments and analyse data. After teaching all day he would rush to his practice and give therapy sessions to his clients long into the night. Balancing academia with therapy, alongside the responsibilities of a young family, was challenging.

The time pressures meant everything was barely held together as he stretched himself thinly to meet the punishing demands of academia, a small business, clients care and raising a family. None was ever done to the high standard he wished for.

GEOFF ALSO FOUND THAT THE ROLE of spirituality in mental health tended to not be a major area of interest for many funding bodies, or universities, or his academic colleagues.

His commitment to it severely hindered his opportunities to attract research funds, work in high-calibre research teams and conduct scientific studies. Often he would fund his own research privately through the earnings of his psychology practice. To him it was worth it.

An added pressure was his interest in spirituality itself. A commitment to a spiritual life requires time. Students need to read spiritual material and some level of spiritual practice must be maintained. Meditations, prayers, rituals all need to fit in somewhere and, like any occupation, professional development courses need to be attended. Certainly, things would have been easier if he had dropped spirituality all together and dedicated his career to more common psychology topics like anxiety or depression. Life, he thought, would be so simple if he could just focus on psychology.

SHORTLY AFTER OPENING HIS PRACTICE Geoff experienced a period of immense spiritual development that went beyond anything he had experienced with yoga.

During his meditations he began having visions of shamans, of eagles, and lands filled with canyons and deserts. On a few rare instances those visions were coupled with body tremors and seizures and his body would be thrown to the floor and pulse with energy.

At other times, he would move into trance and spontaneously dance to a rhythm unheard by anyone but him. His dreams also became routes to adventure. Occasionally his wife would be woken by his singing, loudly, in his sleep — in foreign languages. These experiences went far beyond anything he'd encountered in psychology and even his yoga mentors had little comment on or advice about how to interpret what was happening to him.

BECAUSE HE WAS TRAINED in the assessment of abnormal psychology, Geoff knew his experiences were not pathological but, rather, transcendental. Geoff had started exploring shamanism — the most ancient of spiritual practices — all the while keeping his experiences secret from his academic and professional colleagues. Most of his colleagues did not even meditate let alone fly with eagles into spirit worlds.

It was his study of shamanism, the most ancient of spiritual approaches, that provided what he needed. Over a couple of years, Geoff participated in various courses with Australian shamanic healers and was opened to a whole new world of spirituality, one that felt refreshingly free of religious dogma, scriptures and rules.

Through his exploration of shamanic healing he met like-minded men and women: People deeply concerned with the health of Mother Earth and the dangers of the consumerist culture fuelling the climate crisis. These were new friends who valued modern medicine but also held a deep respect for traditional wisdom and traditional healing methods. He could truly be himself with these people and learnt a new way of being present in the world.

THE SHAMANIC HEALERS HE MET used different approaches to the therapeutic relationship than those practising psychology. Psychologists, generally, are trained to have strong boundaries, which helps them remain objective and ensures the therapeutic work stays focused on the client. Physical touch, like a therapist-to-client hug, for example, is discouraged. It crosses a client-therapist boundary and opens the door to other boundary violations possibly even of a sexual nature. The shamanic healers he trained with, however had what psychologists would consider "loose boundaries" where they would share their personal stories and treat their clients to healing hugs as respected brothers and sisters.

This validated Geoff's ideals and taught him that being real and authentic was an essential part of the healing process and with it came safety, security and trust. It was nurturing and also a sign of respect for the client.

The most valuable lessons he learned in his study were the importance of community, of owning and sharing your life story, and the power of a heartfelt hug. Contrary to what he might have thought when entering, it was those human elements and considerations, and not the mysticism, the spirituality, and healing rituals, that resonated most loudly.

Psychologists use talking therapy with their clients. It's a powerful way to help a person articulate and understand their thoughts, emotions and life processes and happens through a combination of counselling, skills training (e.g. teaching a person communication methods) and problem solving. There are many different types of talking therapies and psychologists train for many years to be qualified to use them. Over time, while continuing his training in talking therapies, Geoff's abilities as a healer increased. He began to understand and use the energy of the body to heal. It was a requirement of his shamanic healing training to provide healing sessions and, with their permission, Geoff offered them to a select group of clients. They were made fully aware of the processes before they received the healings and agreed that Geoff would gather their feedback.

THE FIRST HEALINGS THROUGH THE LENS of shamanic healing had mixed results. Clients would sometimes report little or no effect. The feedback left Geoff feeling confused, even foolish. There were others, however, who reported strange bodily sensations during the healings and also a noted reduction in their levels of stress. This, and other positive signs, encouraged him to continue.

Geoff began integrating different techniques into his healings — the use of percussion (drumming, rattles), singing and hands-on energy healing (channelling energy through the hands into the client). He renewed his meditation process which had the dual benefit of deepening his own connection with the divine (a practice that had waned with the competing demands of his work and family commitments) and being useful to his clients. The turning point in his treatments came with the use of sound and hands-on healing. Clients reported significant reductions in distress, as well as floating sensations, warm currents and waves of sound moving through them, and dark energy oozing out of their body. With his healing abilities strengthened to such a degree, he was confident of openly providing 'spiritual healing' services.

An interesting dilemma arose, however, within months of Geoff beginning to offer his spiritual healing sessions. As a professional psychologist, Geoff had the strong, science-based training as part of his 'toolkit'. And because psychology is a science, psychologists are directed to use only therapies that have been proven effective through scientific research. Indeed, it can be seen as unethical to provide unproven treatments to clients without clear justification, and many insurance agencies and government bodies mandate psychologists use only scientific evidence-based treatments. While he is in complete accord with this and thinks it sensible, there were times when Geoff felt the directives were too restrictive. He wanted to expand his healing repertoire for the times when the evidence-based treatments were not effective.

THE PRACTICE OF HEALING is not done in isolation. Therapeutic communities provide professional support; places for sharing experiences, techniques and further training — all highly valued. There were some in his professional community, however, who questioned his decisions to explore, train in and use treatment methods — shamanism, sound healing and energy medicine — they considered 'fanciful'. There were especially vocal about the lack of empirical evidence to support these modalities' effectiveness. Ironically, that was the very research evidence that Geoff was trying to produce. As well as that, he had first-hand experience and evidence from client feedback that his methods worked. He and they thought it worth exploring further.

It was not an easy road to travel. It might have been easier option for Geoff to provide only evidence-based talk therapies. He would then not be vulnerable to the inevitable resistance, even ridicule, from traditional psychologists.

Or, he could continue exploring spiritual therapies. Geoff knew he was one of the few clinical psychologists with personal experiences in these domains as well as the academic skills to research them. So, he made a choice and decided on a holistic approach. He never abandoned the evidence-based therapies that he knew were highly effective. He also chose a broader range of therapies whenever he could. His patients were increasingly not only interested in, but asking for, the energy work. Interestingly, there were times when his clients got angry when the more spiritually based therapies were not used, and insisted on them. It felt like a waste, and even an offence, to turn his back on an ancient healing approach, with which he had somehow been gifted. He'd studied it, formally or informally, for years. He had suffered a loss of academic advancement from his commitment to a 'fringe' area that few in his profession supported. But he was not stopping.

GEOFF'S OVERALL HEALING METHOD — holistic — means clients

are encouraged to look at the physical, mental and spiritual dimensions of their lives. They're guided to modify their nutrition if it is not optimal, consider meditation if they've not used the technique to date and receive other complementary modalities such as energy healing, sound healing and hypnotherapy as part of their sessions and ongoing work. Those with a religious background are encouraged to practise their faith. Those that are spiritually-inclined are encouraged to explore and deepen this. All clients are encouraged to connect with the healing tools of Mother Earth — the land, nature and their community. All clients receive the same respect and care and this means that nothing in his healing practices is mandatory. Rather, Geoff explains the process of the alternate healing modalities and invites clients to decide what their sessions will be.

Geoff's pathway through life mirrors the difficulties that many young people face; particularly those at a crossroads not knowing where to go. So many young people today struggle to identify their paths. Parents, invariably wanting the best for their children, can often exacerbate the children's distress by pressuring them to find a career direction. Geoff experienced this sense of lostness, himself. He took many years to find even a beginning, any direction, and with continual enquiry and study, a clear path emerged.

It's Geoff's inspired and inspiring journey, that reassures us that there is always reason to hope that the pathway will clear itself.

CHAPTER SEVEN
BODY AND SOUL

*Communicate, even when it's uncomfortable or uneasy.
One of the best ways to heal is simply getting everything out.*

— UNKNOWN

THE WEEK BEFORE CHRISTMAS, I suffered another health setback. My usual festive preparations were non-existent. My intense fear of public places had made Christmas shopping impossible for me. Chris was left to buy gifts and everything else we needed.

A brave attempt to visit to my hairdresser, Lilli, turned into a traumatic experience. Lilli, always supportive and caring, talked me through my panic attack while cutting and styling my hair. I stared at myself in the mirror while she chatted away, and only saw pain and confusion. The room had started spinning. Then, my usual urge to escape, to run outside, surged. Voices of passers-by reverberated in my ears. I had to get back to safety. Call Chris. His voice, reassuring and calm eased the rising panic while Lilli manoeuvred herself around my erratic movements.

Our house, usually bustling with excitement, featured only a sparsely decorated Christmas tree. Rolls of Christmas wrapping and sheets of gift tags sat unopened. I'd missed out on the bustle of the shopping mall, the secret wrapping and the excitement of hiding gifts for the kids. Our family tradition, one I started when Sasha was born — three wrapped gifts for each person — was in danger of slipping.

On Christmas eve, I woke up with a pain in my left leg. By the afternoon it had become unbearable. Chris insisted I go to the hospital to have it checked out. Once again, without warning, my life was thrown into disarray.

The emergency room, filled with worried looking people, was the last place anyone wanted to be at any given time, let alone Christmas Eve. A few seats away from me, a young couple with two toddlers and a baby, caught my attention. The woman, hunched over in agony, a canular inserted in her right arm, waited to be admitted to a ward. Her partner was cuddling the baby, and struggling to keep the toddlers in their seats. *What will their Christmas be like?*

Behind me a young man helped an older man to complete hospital admission forms to change details because his sister, his next of kin, was currently in jail. A young woman rushed in crying, doubled over in pain, fearing a miscarriage.

After blood tests and further examination, the young doctor on duty, broke the news of a suspected deep vein thrombosis (DVT) and said I should be admitted as a precaution. Two years earlier, I'd been diagnosed with a DVT and now it seemed to still be there.

The doctor kneeled next to me, and tried to alleviate my fears before wishing me well for Christmas. Chris, exhausted after a long day at work, left to attend midnight Mass.

The sound of beeping heart monitors and snoring patients filled the festively decorated ward. Nursing staff moved around doing patient observations. I was relieved, in a sense, that sleep evaded me. My dreams would not arrive.

For first time in my life I missed midnight Mass. I searched on YouTube for recordings and listened through my headphones. Around me, dark shadows lurked, and I could not contain my anxiety. In the quiet night, I wept.

The next morning, during an ultrasound, I suffered a full-blown panic attack. It started building when the young man, who directed my bed out of the ward knocked into the wall. This triggered my fear of falling. The radiographer, gently talked me through the episode until he was able to perform the procedure. A definite diagnosis of a DVT in my left leg was made. Straight onto blood thinners, and discharged Christmas afternoon, I left with an urgent appointment for a haematologist two days later.

SASHA, MICHELIN, LISA and our grandchildren were waiting at home, ready for me to open my presents. I tried to join in the excitement but I was exhausted. I couldn't even think of answering the many phone messages. I needed sleep, peaceful sleep.

By that time, I'd already started counting the days to my next appointment with Geoff. Even from only one visit, therapy felt easier than I had expected. I was also desperate for solutions and thought I'd get them from him. The room's walls held a deep spirituality tucked in their crevices. As Geoff discussed clinical strategies, an energy of calm and a deep peace surrounded him. His gentle manner, akin to the atmosphere in the room, soothed me.

On the window sill a stick of incense glowed — energy-clearing sage filled the room. I prayed for a good session, one with no tears, where I could talk through at least some of my troubles. He always looked at me with such kindness when I explained my medical woes.

'How do you feel about what's happened to you?' Geoff asked.

'I always worry the doctors are missing something,' I lamented. 'I feel unwell all the time. But they can't find anything wrong with me, until the DVT, recently.'

If he thought that I was a hypochondriac, he did not show it.

I was so nervous about giving Geoff a copy of *A Darker Shade of Pale*, I started second-guessing myself. *Am I divulging too much? Will it help him to form a clinical opinion of me? Would he see how my habits and behaviours came from my childhood trauma?* He *is* a psychologist. It has to offer him insight into my background, doesn't it?

There were so many things to talk about. The things I wrote about in my book — oppression, our grief, and harassment. So much. And just an hour.

The pressure was intense. Details of my childhood trauma, now alive and running my mind. It seemed so far from my current life. But the pain was as fresh as if it happened yesterday: Watching Owen on the ground while they pumped water out of his body, waiting for him to sit up and smile; the crushing sound of the tractor as my young neighbourhood friend lay buried under its weight. Why did they not spare us that sight when they removed his body? We were 10. I wanted to discuss how personally I took it all; explain that I feel like a bad person and walk around with shame. The world doesn't feel safe and it feels like no one can help me.

I UNDERSTOOD THAT FEAR, loneliness and isolation never left me alone and were holding me back. I'd sit staring at the numbers calling my phone without responding. In the throes of a panic attack, I'd fear that the pressure would escalate and never leave me.

The same questions came. Why is this happening? Why do I feel like this? Why is happiness evading me? And one played all the time. What is wrong with me?

I wanted to ask other questions but there was never enough time. Who am I outside of this pain? Who would I be if I started living my life outside of my story?

'Is it possible to put things in the past where they belong?' I asked.

'Yes, it is possible,' he said.

I jumped in. 'How?'

'It needs to be spoken through in counselling, in detail, and sometimes several times over so that you can process all the material and take the emotional charge out of it.' He sounded reassuring.

'But I struggle with … with talking about it,' I said.

'Of course. Dealing with trauma is complex because people may not remember the details, or find them hard to think about… talk about. Psychologists help people overcome this,' he explained.

'Sometimes I feel like I create my reality around trauma. How do I change it? Can I allow it to pass naturally?'

'This is what we're addressing in these sessions. Talking about it is usually enough in itself to address some of the emotion in the story,' he explained. 'And yes, in some cases, you need to explore events from multiple perspectives so you can release the emotion. That can also change how you've perceived the event. We are exploring this.'

'Is it possible to stop attracting trauma?' I asked.

'The idea that we attract trauma is very controversial,' he said.

'But I feel constantly under threat. And I really am accident prone and that makes things so much more traumatic.'

'There are theories that we attract what we unconsciously believe. Not all professionals agree. But if we assume people do attract trauma it's because they think they deserve it. They attract persecution in some form… stay a victim. Or they put themselves in danger to attract trauma.' He looked at me and added. 'If they change the unconscious beliefs, they can stop attracting trauma.'

'I feel like I'm cursed,' I said. 'Things happen to me, some of them really traumatic physically and emotionally, I want it to stop'.

'Surely you don't believe that, do you?' he said with such gentleness that I felt the tears welling up.

'I don't know what to believe any more,' I wailed. 'I'm the one who'd step into a lift holding a small baby and spark a rescue mission, walk into someone's office to deliver something and attract a stalker; or step on a piece of ice and end up in the emergency room.'

Geoff reached for the tissues and gave me his deeply comforting gaze. When I'd stopped talking, he talked or drew diagrams and asked questions. I'd only be half listening because I was distracted by his books. *Should I ask him whether I have PTSD?*

I wanted a diagnosis, something I could process, deconstruct and solve. I couldn't tell him I wanted to Google the symptoms and work on fixing myself.

'What do you think is wrong with me,' I blurted out. 'I need a diagnosis.'

This time his gaze was elsewhere. He hesitated and I kept observing him carefully. *Why's he looking the other way?*

'Isn't it important to have a diagnosis so healing can happen?' I urged.

'A diagnosis is a label for categorising symptoms,' he replied. 'It's not necessary to have one, to work on yourself. What is though, for me, is to cultivate a good relationship with you and to gain your trust so that together we work on managing your mental illness.'

Mental illness. The words terrified me. I didn't want him to see that so I kept babbling, but my mind built the scenario of an out-of-control crazy woman.

'I need to know what's wrong, the causes and how to manage my symptoms,' I said.

'Your doctor referred you with generalised anxiety and panic disorder. That's just a generic diagnosis for when excessive worry interferes with concentration and daily activity,' he said. 'But underlying it is complex trauma and grief. That's the psychological material that all that harassment activated.'

'So, can I fix that?' I pleaded. 'I have to find myself; I'm lost somewhere. I don't want to continue living this way. I need new ways to cope with my anxiety so I can finally heal. I've carried this, this burden all my life,' I wailed.

He gently pushed the tissue box closer.

'I'm lost, I'm in the dark wilderness and I can't find my way back,' I sobbed. 'I don't want anyone to see me this way. You know, people have expectations of me to be a certain way.'

'Is that why you don't want to go out in public,' he prodded.

'I can't go out there, I'm afraid something will happen,' I said.

'Can you tell me what you think will happen?'. He spoke softly.

'I won't be able to find my way. I can't concentrate. I'm struggling to write. I'm such a failure.' I cried. 'It's like I've landed in a new country and I have to learn a new language.'

During these outbursts Geoff would gently soothe me by talking me through the moment. Anxiety, panic disorder and depression are not things we can see or grab hold of. That made it harder for me to understand. Once my fear took hold, I had to abandon my fight against the new understanding and let it pass.

He was truly patient. He listened to the struggle I had with my negativity, my inclination to self-sabotage and hypervigilance.

'Some of the common symptoms people struggle with are constant worry, or stress or low mood. They can interfere with how one functions daily: at work, in relationships, at leisure or how they take care of themselves,' he said.

'I was born a worrier, you know. And I guess I've become more of a worrier as I've grown older,' I said.'

'Some ways these symptoms manifest are through a struggle with managing your emotions. These can present through behaviours, like overeating, drinking too much, smoking more than normal, using drugs, gambling or sex. Other signs that people often ignore include thoughts of hopelessness, worthlessness or lack of motivation, lack of sleep or need for excessive sleep. Thoughts about death, dying or suicide … that's a strong sign,' he explained.

'For years, I successfully buried my symptoms; actually, thought I could manage them,' I said. 'I wish I'd sought help a lot earlier. Things would have been so different.'

'That's not unusual,' he said. 'And definitely not something you should beat yourself up about. In your case, being very avoidant of people and panic attacks are clear warning signs that you need help'.

IN TRUTH, THE PEOPLE CLOSEST TO ME — Chris, Sasha and Michelin — couldn't understand my level of despair. For years, I'd been managing. I was the captain of my ship and steered it in any direction that pleased me. A successful, independent, go-getter who'd now cracked. My brain, which had carried, but buried, the heavy load was now exploding.

In addition, the incessant worry about my health sank me further. Then, at times, I didn't know myself. What was I worrying about? I was usually the problem solver, it's what I excelled at. Now, I found complications. Not a solution in sight. I was exhausted. I detested my anxiety and wanted to strangle it.

'Do you ever speak to your anxiety?' asked Geoff.

'Yes, I scream at it when I it orders me to stand or sit or shake or squirm. That's when I can't *stop* shaking,' I said. '

'Well, I suggest you are brutal in confronting the anxiety, instruct it to go away. Be brutal,' he repeated.

'Sometimes I think anxiety creeps into my head at night and that's why I can't sleep. Or it creeps in when I am in the car waiting for the light to change,' I said.

A sweet smile from Geoff.

'And now, right before I have to speak at an event it rears its ugly head. Is that anxiety or panic disorder?' I asked.

'Anxiety is a normal human response,' he said. 'It's got a job. That's to keep us aware of and protected from danger. It's something we'll always have. But the challenge is to learn to turn down the volume. Take it from an abnormal to a normal level.'

'You know, I've really got everything … most things I've dreamed of. A loving family, we've travelled the world, a great career, lived my producer's dream to heights I would never have imagined. I am grateful, so grateful for my life and how much I've achieved. And, at the same time, I feel like a failure.'

I turned to face him. 'Please tell me I'm not crazy.'

'No, you are *not* crazy, but constant worry is driving you crazy.' He spoke with such gentleness that I felt tears slip down my cheek.

'What do you do when you start feeling unsettled?' he asked.

'I usually pace around. I try to reason with myself,' I replied. What I didn't add, though I don't know why, was that even though I knew the unsettled feeling was the one I had to let run through me and then I'd be able to calm myself. What I also didn't add is that when I'm on that rollercoaster, no amount of reasoning helps.

CHAPTER EIGHT
CULTIVATING PEACE

Tragedy should be utilised as a source of strength. No matter what sort of difficulties, how painful experience is, if we lose our hope, that's our real disaster.

— His Holiness, the Dalai Lama

'ONE OF THE PRACTICES I can suggest is putting your thoughts down in writing or calming yourself with meditation', he said.

I was about to answer, but spotted the time on the clock. The hour had passed. At the thought of going home and facing my life again, my legs started shaking uncontrollably and my breathing quickened. I was scared I'd pass out. *Breathe slowly, I willed myself. In for five, hold for four and out for six.* I was trying hard to control my shaking body, but the room started closing in on me.

'Come with me,' he said softly. His voice sounded far away as if he was in another room and not sitting opposite me.

In the large room, he quickly set up the portable bed. I needed to rest my body and the bed offered my weak limbs some respite.

'Let's practice some meditation to try and calm yourself, if that's OK with you,' he said.

Eager to stop the racing thoughts and relieved to be off my trembling legs, I stared at the ceiling. Darkness hovered above, my rapid breathing caused a dizziness and my racing pulse sent vibrations throughout my body. Rigid limbs, fists clenched, I tried hard to slow my breath and to take in the aroma of the incense.

'Close your eyes, I want you to think of your ancestors, picture them and draw on their strength.'

My mind drifted to my father's family. I had never met my grandparents on either side of our family. I wondered what my paternal grandmother would have looked like. I pictured her as tall, with white hair like my Dad's. In the stillness, a mental image of someone I had never seen, not even in a photograph, appeared. I willed her, no pleaded with her to help me find strength to overcome my fears. I longed for *her* strength, and wondered about her struggles as a slave on the island where she bore children. I'd read that the legacy of trauma can be passed through generations. Now thoughts about the harrowing experiences my grandparents faced as slaves swirled in my mind.

My maternal grandmother birthed 16 children, including two sets of twins, and ran her household with resilience. Mum, had six children, struggled as the breadwinner of our family and, at 89, is still showing such strength. *What about me?* Tears rolled down my face as thoughts of my perceived weakness to fight this condition surfaced.

In the stillness, my mind continued to search for a connection to my ancestors. Geoff's movements, softened by the soft sound of singing bowls, were hardly audible. These bowls, also known as Himalayan bowls, are used in various healing modalities including yoga, music therapy, and sound healing. When the bowl is struck with a wooden mallet, the tone rises and the bowl is said to be singing. The sounds generated from Tibetan bowls promote a type of energy medicine; known to heal sufferers from many mental health disorders, many other diseases.

The hypnotic sound had an instant calming effect. The soft tone relaxed my mind as the vibrations spread through my body. The tension in my shoulders eased, allowing me to cradle my head in the soft pillows, releasing the muscles in my face and neck. Creating this type of moment, takes great effort. In this sacred space, surrounded by the soothing sounds, an atmosphere of tranquillity settled around me. In that moment, the heaviness and darkness drained from my body, escaping through my pores, the tips of my fingers, the top of my head; and drifted away. Floating on a soft cloud, my breathing slowed, allowing my mind to let go and release the built-up anxious thoughts.

A radiant light infiltrated my cells, allowing my eyeballs to relax while my hands lay gently on my belly. The healing aroma of the incense filled my nostrils; I breathed in every morsel.

When Geoff's hands cradled my head. I prayed to my ancestors. His hands rested on my knee close to the DVT and then held my feet.

The sound of a loud drum startled me. In deep relaxation, I felt the urge to open my eyes to experience the sight as the healing rhythm filled the space. I'm not sure how long the meditation and healing took but I did not want it to end. When the chant signalled the end of the healing session, the room held a renewed energy.

'Take your time to open your eyes and come back now,' I heard his soft voice in the distance.

No. I don't want to open my eyes. It's so peaceful here. But slowly I opened my eyes to look up at the ceiling. The darkness that always hovered over me, taunting me, slowly closing in and wrapping itself around my me, had disappeared into the rafters. Exhaling a sigh of relief, smiling, I looked over to see Geoff sitting on a rolled-up pillow.

'Thank you,' I mumbled. 'This was beautiful.'

'Let's look at a date for your next appointment,' he said.

AN UNBELIEVABLE PEACE SURROUNDED ME. *Please don't let this be a dream.* Everything seemed so normal, so light, as if my mind had been switched to a slower tempo. I felt a strength in my arms and legs. *Am I healed? Is this all I needed?*

On the drive home it was hard to relay to Chris what I had just experienced. He wanted to stop for coffee but in this tranquil state I wanted to get home, sit on the deck and savour the moment.

With this renewed energy, later that night, I sat at my computer to work on my manuscript. It was already overdue and I'd promised my editor to have it to her soon. In the last few months my poor concentration had stalled my writing. The many unopened emails caught my attention. Opening the emails drew me back into the vile, disgusting messages from online trolls, filled with words belittling my lineage and book. There were comments from others who felt that I was not worthy of writing a book about life in South Africa during apartheid. *Who are you? Where are you from? What did you ever do for the anti-apartheid movement?*

'You ran away,' one person claimed. 'Now you are writing about South Africa from your cushy new country. Just who do you think you are.'

Shattered by these personal and insensitive comments about my lineage, the dark shadows danced around me, taunting me to embrace its energy. Determined not to let this unsettle me, I turned to meditation hoping to connect with my spirit animal to protect me.

Several hours later I crawled into bed. A terrible flood filled my dreams. I was drowning. Chris tried to save me but he couldn't hold onto my hand. Round and round I tossed until Chris's voice and my violent shaking brought me back from this nightmare hell.

Later, wandering around the house, I wanted to contact Geoff to ask him how to bring myself back to the sacred space he had created. But it was nearly midnight. The six days to my next therapy session come soon enough.

MY RITUAL OF MEDITATION, prayer, walking and sitting on the deck got me through most days. In addition, weekly therapy sessions and short periods of writing offered relief from the darkness. My car, parked in the driveway beckoned, only I did not have the courage to get behind the wheel.

'Are you getting enough sleep, Geoff asked. 'You look tired. Your eyes look dull.'

'No, I'm not,' I answered. 'I have these recurring dreams, every night. They scare me because it's always about disasters.'

'Please don't tell anybody about this or don't write it in your notes. I don't want anyone to know,' I quickly added.

'I promise you whatever you tell me stays in this room,' he said.

'Are you sure you don't have to write a report to my doctor as a follow-up? I asked.

'I promise you no one will know what you tell me during these sessions,' he said looking directly at me. 'The only time that I would need to divulge information is when I feel that you are a danger to yourself.'

'You mean suicidal,' I added. 'You don't have to fear that from me.'

He nodded.

'I don't know how to stop these dreams,' I cried. 'They fill me with such terror.'

These conversations would lead to more in-depth discussions about my fears and what writing the book had unearthed. My thoughts, continually zoned in on my past trauma, charged my emotions into overload. The confrontation with someone from high school had triggered these feelings of insecurity and the continual reminders of the dehumanising experience of apartheid ruminated. *How do I stop these thoughts?*

'Untreated chronic anxiety and panic disorder disrupts the energy flow in your body, he said. 'Disruptions to your diet and sleeping pattern and general wellbeing will provoke a bigger imbalance in your mental state. What is your diet like? Can you improve that?'

'I have so many food intolerances, I said. 'You wouldn't want me as a dinner guest.'

In recent months I had developed many food intolerances. My limited diet and lack of nutritious food led to low energy levels. Thankfully Chris and Sasha regularly prepared meals from the list of foods I could tolerate to help me stay nourished.

'Is there a way I can live outside of this fear?' I asked.

'Fear is a central human reaction and it can be quite helpful to keep your life on track,' Geoff offered reassuringly.

Only I could not see a life filled with deep meaning and contentment while fear was ever present. I craved a life where I could cultivate joy, peace and calmness and radiance. This was the life I wanted to wake up to each morning and be eternally grateful for a new day.

During these discussions, Geoff would reach for his notepad and pen to illustrate how an imbalance of my mental state would impact my general wellbeing. Using lines, columns, arrows, and words he'd clarify my mental confusion and where I was at.

'You mean like being on a never-ending merry-go-round until I can no longer stand up,' I said.

'Something like that,' he nodded.

So many childhood traumas, long buried, had opened up like an active volcano waiting to erupt. Geoff sat quietly, listening as I unleashed some of my past history and pain. These topics, a trigger for my anxiety, would leave me trembling, making it difficult to swallow and struggling to bring things under control.

An intense longing for my active lifestyle, left me fretting about finding my way back. Public places had become my worst trigger for racing pulse and fear of falling. The harsh lights in shopping centres impacted my vision and the noise in crowded places left me fearful. Chris never complained or put pressure on me to stay and sit it out. In fact, he wanted to shield me from these experiences by encouraging me to stay home. The more pressure I put on myself, the harder it became to do things that others seemingly did with ease.

'Geoff, I miss my independence,' I'd cry. 'I feel helpless, trapped. I can't accept that this is my life now. I'm trying so hard to sit behind the wheel of my car or to walk into a shop.'

'It will happen,' he constantly reassured me.

We'd discuss varying scenarios to help me beat my fears. This person — who I'd thought was too young and inexperienced — surprised me with his wisdom. He looked at me incredulously at times when I talked about my busy work schedule. Whenever he rolled his eyes, clenched his jaw or avoided my eyes, my resistance would rise and self-pity would surface. *Who does he think he is? This therapy is a mistake, he doesn't understand my problems.*

Therapy sessions now became my escape from the daily pain and ruminating thoughts. And Geoff was now in the firing line. I wanted to lash out at those who'd oppressed me, my family and blame them for shaping my life, for sucking out my natural soul's journey, destroying my right to a normal life. I wanted a life where I didn't have to walk a few steps behind them and wait for their handouts.

Geoff and I, the unlikeliest match, had somehow come together in a healing centre in Sutherland bushland. I'm sure when I first arrived at his practice, he had no idea of the turbulent sessions we would encounter. Sessions where he would sit across from me while I unleashed my anger towards white supremacy, towards the oppressors and what they stood for. He resembled them. In my frustration at times, when I looked at him, I'd unleash torrents of words that were harsh, unfair and inappropriate. At times I had to rephrase a sentence for clarity. But, as a true professional, he allowed me to unleash my pain, while he offered only kindness.

And so, the therapy cycle continued. What I liked about working with Geoff was that he constantly challenged me. His throwaway lines, at times angered me, but ultimately it set me on the path to thinking about things in a different way. Many times, during therapy, I wanted to lash out at him for asking a pertinent question I was unwilling to answer. Or for continuing to probe when I wanted to stop. But most weeks I'd leave his rooms ready to tackle the week and to work on the strategies we discussed.

The healing sessions, those moments when I could let go of the battle raging inside me, always left me feeling refreshed, calm and filled with a renewed strength. The combination of talk therapy and healing sessions instilled a sense of optimism about the future. The beating of the drum, the rattlers, the smell of sage incense and singing bowls filled me with a deep peace. My mind usually drifted to the place where I wanted to be. Right there fulfilling my destiny.

CHAPTER NINE
THERAPY, HEALING

*You can only experience true healing when
the mind and spirit are on the same level.*

— Dr Geoff Lyons

UNDER GEOFF'S GUIDANCE, I was able to meditate for longer periods between therapy sessions. Meditation offered an escape from the chaos in my mind, another survival technique. I had a renewed sense of purpose.

At every session, armed with a new diagram and coping strategies, he helped me recognise my negative thoughts and work on changing them. The big room, always dimly lit, became my sacred space of healing. Being receptive and open to his healing energy strengthened my spirit.

'You can only experience true healing when the mind and spirit are on the same level,' he said. 'When you address both these elements then powerful life transformations can happen.'

WHILE THERE WAS A GOOD DEAL of progress being made, some things were not as comfortable or, indeed, comforting as they might have been.

'My family are smothering me with love and support,' I said, one session, 'and it makes me uncomfortable.'

'Well, it must be hard for them to see you in such despair,' he said.

'I understand,' I replied. 'But I feel moody, a lot of the time and just want to be left alone. I think they worry when that happens ... because it's not like me.'

One weekend, when Sasha was away, and he had to work on an urgent project, Chris arranged for Michelin to stay with me. I was frustrated by that; I wanted to move closer to being independent. Geoff did not take sides but rather looked at solution, and offered a suggestion for how I might defuse my anger and frustration by subtly suggesting I take control of the situation.

'Why not tell Michelin to go home early, then go to the store, buy some ingredients and cook something? What about preparing a special meal,' he said?

Perplexed, I stared at him and nearly burst out laughing. *Good grief, I've been married for such a long time, does he know how many specials meals I've cooked?*

It was not easy to be calm at that point. But I found myself doing just what he had suggested. Baking bread and cooking something special soon became like an escape and not a chore. It developed into a 'go-to' solution whenever the darkness engulfed me. It became my creative time, and often, while mixing batter or chopping onions, I had the deepest conversations with myself.

To my surprise, these activities revealed many gifts I'd been too busy to recognise and appreciate. My spatula and mixing bowl became a feature on the kitchen bench, and beckoned when negativity surfaced. There was something comforting and calming in mixing dough, kneading it and watching the bread rise in the oven. This slower pace settled my jitters. I had always been too busy creating for a purpose and had never thought about doing this as therapy.

My weekly sessions now had the element of positivity which made it somewhat easier to admit to the negative aspects. Yet, my push for perfectionism still circled. During a particularly bad week I had become downhearted about my lack of continual positive thoughts. Eager to let him see my progress, I exaggerated some of my progress.

I longed for Geoff to say, 'You are cured, go forth and live'. However, I sensed he could see right through my façade. This frustrated me even more. Too much intuition for one person.

One diagram of Geoff's I didn't approve of, showed me in the centre of a circle with many rings around it. The rings represented the outside pressures caving in on me, crushing me. *Did he know who he was talking to?* The queen of busy schedules. If I didn't have work to do, I'd create an event just to keep the adrenaline flowing. The standing joke in our family is that when I start a sentence with 'I've been thinking,' they all scatter and hide. It always means it's all hands-on deck to pull off a project.

With the publication of *A Darker Shade of Pale*, most waking moments were spent writing and rewriting. The rush of excitement about completion and, ultimately, the publication propelled me. My already busy schedule now included book launches, travel and media interviews, my annual charity ball, and community events.

THIS CRAZY MOMENTUM has been my life for as long as I can remember. When I arrived in Australia, after settling Sasha and Michelin in school, I hit the employment rollercoaster. Never content with just one job, I routinely looked for additional projects. I grasped every single opportunity. No one around me realised how hard I had to work to satisfy *myself* that I was good enough.

I somehow managed, even when I'd been thrown in at the deep end, to survive and work things out. I thrived on pressure and everyone commented on my calm demeanour. Yet, more than anyone knew, I escaped to my office or the bathroom for more tile counting, to relieve the pressure. There was little time left for mental health care. What seemed, then, to be my way of boosting my mental state was working and proving myself. That kept my anxious thoughts of failure buried under the layers.

Working on some of the major events in the state left me buzzing, boosted my confidence and set off ideas of eventually doing my own events. I was driven by the adrenaline rush of events like the Sydney 2000 Olympics and Paralympic Games, and the Sydney 2002 Gay Games. I wished my Dad, so passionate about sport, was still alive. This would have been a highlight for him. *If he could only see me now.*

Working at the Medal Ceremonies at the Olympic Games in 2000, was a dream come true. Interacting with elite athletes and dignitaries in that atmosphere was exhilarating; any fears I had of failing and any worrying health conditions were easily pushed aside when I had goals in my sight.

MANY YEARS AGO, I found out that something that can be a curse, can also be a blessing. Failure was my nemesis. But it was also, the start of one of my most successful ventures. One of my first tasks when I was seconded to work on Sydney 2002 Gay Games, was to help a choir from Cape Town be part of the Cultural Festival. Despite my best efforts, however, I failed miserably to help them. Every possible funding avenue was declined and attempts to raise money from the diaspora also failed. It was out of this failure that the idea was borne to help previously disadvantaged entertainers from my home town to come to Australia. I registered a new business: Beryl Segers Presents.

I was spurred on by the enthusiasm of the diaspora, and set about creating entertainment to remind us of a bygone era. I now had another race to run. Late nights, tour schedules, community projects, contract negotiations, lengthy phone calls, and paperwork, lots of paperwork. All the while I held down a demanding full-time job.

I remained in the backroom setting everything in place for everyone else to enjoy. It gave me a great sense of achievement to see artists landing in Australia and igniting the community with their talent.

When I also formed a community theatre production company, I was spreading my time even thinner, however, bringing to life some of my favourite musicals and working with talented local artists and production enthusiasts was thrilling.

For the next 18 years, I juggled all these projects, jumping from one event to another without regard for my own wellbeing or whether they were financially viable. Higher and higher, each event more challenging, more creative.

'How are you going to top this one,' appreciative supporters regularly asked.

This encouraged me to make the next event bigger and more challenging than the last. Soon I included New Zealand as part of the itinerary and juggled my leave at work to deliver the tours.

The community support reinforced my enthusiasm to continue with charitable projects to support in South Africa. I thrived on helping others. desperate to boost the fragile sense of self-worth that had manifested in my childhood. Stay busy, think less about the pain. But now, I found out that something that can be a blessing, can also be a curse. I had succumbed to the relentless pressure and seemed to have lost my way.

In previous years my creativity had kept me going when panic overwhelmed me. When I panicked about dying, or someone dying in my family I was more keenly aware of out-of-control moments. I couldn't stop the anxiety pumping through my body so I couldn't calm myself. No amount of breathing or self-talk would work. I had to let it run its course. My usual logical way of thinking vanished as my mind seemed to close in and guard against more hopelessness in the face of the randomness of my life. I was vigilant for any hint of danger. It was crippling and exhausting.

One incident around that time, happened during the most stressful period of my life. From the moment I joined the staff in my new role at a local university, my life somersaulted. I suffered bullying and harassment and then became embroiled with a stalker, had colleagues suffering panic attacks and was present when a close colleague collapsed in my office and suffered an aneurysm.

The incident with the stalker, a mentally ill young man, left me anxious and distressed. He was not deterred by a restraining order issued to the keep him away from our building. For a period, security had to accompany me to the railway station, around campus, and be stationed on my floor. Eventually, the young man was arrested when he sat in the middle of the street outside the building.

On another occasion, on arrival at work, security waited to escort me to another building. After a bullying incident, the faculty management, exercising their duty of care, moved my belongings to a new location overnight. While I was aware of the situation, this sudden move had me worried about my safety.

SO, WHERE HAD THIS ALL BEGUN? My whole life, I had a tendency towards anxiety, but I'd always been able to suppress it, manage it. In 1995, when my sister, Frances, was diagnosed with cancer, I remained strong for her and inwardly fell apart.

Initially her prognosis was to live for 3-6 months. When the specialist rattled off the devastating news, I was with her in the hospital room. Her eyes stayed fixed on my face as he spoke. At that moment, I felt more disturbed by the doctor's appalling bedside manner, than by her prognosis. While I remained strong and supportive of her, I panicked about her dying and that I would suffer a similar fate.

At the time, I was seeing a physiotherapist for unsubstantiated back pain and other symptoms. Many times, I would wait outside his practice to talk to him and that, as well as having him treat me, gave me the support I needed.

Slowly, however, my grief became unbearable. I was still coming to terms with my brother George's sudden death two years prior. So I poured myself into work, my outlet. Always on the go to build this non-stop lifestyle for myself to block everything out. These included, family alcoholism, living under apartheid, moving countries and adjusting to a new life away from everything and everyone I treasured.

My father had died of alcoholism, as had my brother, George, and my antipathy to there being alcohol around anyone I loved, intensified. Where I grew up alcoholism was rife; discrimination broke the spirit of most men in our community. As a child, I'd poured some of my father's alcohol down the sink and added water to his wine. The sight of drunken men repulsed me.

While I don't think most people would label me as having anxiety from the outside, it is now clear that professional success, and appearing to have it together justified my hectic lifestyle to the point of exhaustion. I'd always make everything work and appear with a smile on my face.

After Frances died, I was terrified the same fate awaited me. I had back and breast pain. Imaginary, as it turned out. Losing her was an immense loss of a part of my life that could never be filled again. The strain of her suffering and death also brought a tragic rift in our family. It was a very sad state of events and, had we had access to grief counselling, we could have been able to come together as a family and mourn her loss. The rift continued for the following nine years; nine years in family limbo, with me wondering how she would feel about what was happening in our family.

When I returned to work after her death, my emotions were so out of control that I asked my colleagues not to talk to me about her death. I could not bear to talk about losing her to anyone. I'd have to get up and go to the bathroom to sob. But would return to my desk as if nothing had changed.

I found it nearly impossible to refocus my life, and learn to live with my grief, to live without my siblings. It was a curse, again and, again, a blessing on some level. In many ways it brought me to a deeper sense of knowing myself and to process what had happened.

As usual, instead of building more down-time and calm into my life my solution was to keep running from my anxiety. The deaths of my siblings, starting when Owen drowned, were things I feared my entire life. Constant fear revolved around the causes and timeliness of their deaths. I felt, at times, that my actual memories of them were blocked by their dying.

Many times, my grief was so immense that I thought about the peacefulness of death.

In the first few years of my siblings dying, things were so insane; I was just able to get through. When the shock started wearing off, and reality set in, my anxiety worsened. While my fears were completely logical, it was not unlikely. With George's death, the worst happened for us, and in my mind, no one's destructive behaviour in our family had changed since.

For nearly every positive that happened, I was filled with guilt and regret that I couldn't share it with Frances. I became obsessed about showing more gratitude for the many good things in my life. Then, I was terrified I'd get a call at any minute telling me something else horrifying had happened in our family. This cycle continued, leaving me completely exhausted.

As a child, my little brother Owen's drowning, at the age of four, always left me wondering where he was. Mum and Dad never spoke about him and only placed flowers next to his photograph on the table. My dreams about drowning and struggling under water were so vivid. For years I wanted to dream about Owen, to see him, or for him to show me where he went to. I fantasised about what he would have looked like but the only image I had of him was that of a four-year-old running chasing me around the house and the photograph taken moments before he drowned. I desperately did not want to forget him.

Growing up, whenever tragic events happened in our neighbourhood, I'd replay them for weeks and months after the event.

When I was a child, a tragic accident happened. We children would often run around unsupervised while tractors cleared the vegetation down our street. One afternoon, Errol, my young friend hung onto the back of the tractor, and was crushed to death when he lost his grip. We were 10 years old.

The sight and sound of a tractor terrorised me for years. The confronting visuals of Errol crushed, plagued my memory. All these events had been reawakened during the writing of *A Darker Shade of Pale*.

'Where were you all those years ago when I desperately needed help?' I said to Geoff during a therapy session.

'I wasn't even born yet,' he laughed.

'Do you still meditate?' he asked me during one session.

'Yes, I've been meditating for a while,' I replied. 'I don't know if I'm doing it right, but it feels right. Are you into shamanic healing? I've been exploring that a bit. I'd like to learn more.'

'Yes, I'm trained in shamanism" he replied. 'Though, you need to recognise that there are no absolutes in shamanism. It's just a modern word for traditional, nature-based spirituality that isn't tied to organised religion.'

'I am struggling with religion at the moment,' I said. 'I can't handle the fear that religion pummels into me.'

'Why is that?', he asked.

'While I've always lived a spiritual life, it's taken a battering when things have felt so hopeless,' I said.

'Spirituality is good. Religion can be good too,' he continued 'It's a way people can access spiritual concepts at a simple level. But, yes, some people can find religion very restrictive, narrow-minded and unforgiving. It's not unusual for spiritual people to outgrow those constraints.'

'My lack of interest in religion bothers me,' I said. 'I grew up in a strict Catholic home. It was spirituality that attracted me to your practice. You know… I've experienced a deeply spiritual connection since working with you.'

Then, a question came to me. 'Can you work with someone if they are not spiritual?'

He smiled. 'Well, spirituality is a fundamental part of the human consciousness and people get a much broader and complete therapeutic process when they explore it,' he said.

'How important is spirituality and forgiveness of self to recovery?' I asked. 'Is there a connection?'

'The role of spirituality and forgiveness varies, depending on the person, their situation and the issues they need help with,' he said. 'Forgiveness, for example, is useful if someone's struggling with anger but not if they are depressed, unless they are angry with themselves. Spirituality can provide a rich metaphor, imagery and wisdom that speaks directly to the unconscious.'

It was discussions like these that brought me the comfort I needed. Since I'd started working with Geoff, I sensed he was someone who lived with a foot in both worlds. The spiritual realm and this world. What this did for my spiritual wellbeing was something I had never experienced before.

At times I didn't understand the role spirituality had in my life. The plans I had were, all too often, interrupted by traumatic events. Whenever I talked to God, to Spirit, to the universe, I imagined them laughing at me, squashing my plans.

But I sensed there was something more luminous than religion that I needed. Every morning upon rising, I'd lie down on my yoga mat on the back deck. Headphones on, I'd lose myself in a guided meditation for anxiety and panic with the sound of the birds and the rustling leaves on the trees as my companions. The meditations became my lifelines. Most times I'd lose myself in the tranquillity.

'Tell me,' I said to Geoff one session, 'what is your dream job?'.

'This is my dream job,' he smiled. 'I want to help people with their mental health, not only through clinical methods but holistically and spiritually.'

SOON, TWO MONTHS OF THERAPY had passed and I had made much progress in some areas. But the panic and anxiety were not yet under control. I was reluctant, perhaps scared, to voice my growing frustration and impatience about the slowness of this process, and I continued to work hard on the strategies Geoff offered.

I summoned the courage to talk about my siblings who'd died. When I talked about how much I missed them I invariably cried and cried.

When it came to relating the events, I felt overwhelmed.

At the exact moment that George died, in the middle of the night, I woke up from a deep sleep to call the hospital. He died as I was waiting on the phone. When Frances died, I had just spent the day with her at the hospital. We laughed so much during that visit that I struggled to breathe and she wet herself. The more we laughed, the more we remembered funny stories. A few hours later she was dead. This played over and over in my mind.

'You must remember that you are trying to undo trauma that affected your life a long time ago. It won't be healed overnight,' Geoff said.

'Can trauma ever subside and disappear?' I asked.

'Yes. Traumatic memories can be buried in the mind,' he explained. 'What happens, though, is that once a deeply traumatic thing is experienced, like you being bullied and harassed, it activates all those dormant memories. So with work, like the work we've been doing, all those memories can be processed and the emotional pain of them can subside.'

'I am working so hard and trying everything but I am still struggling so much,' I lamented. 'I miss my siblings. I miss people. I miss my independence. You don't know what it's like. All my projects are stalled. I've got my book to write. I've finally received funding from the local council to start my pet project, a Youth Strings Ensemble. Now I can't.'

Don't cry, Beryl. Don't.

But nothing could stop the tears of frustration, anger, pity and despair from flowing. I couldn't look at him because I didn't want his pity or, Lord forbid, that awkward quiet moment.

At the end of the talk therapy session, Geoff looked at me and suggested we do some energy healing.

'Will you be comfortable on the floor or shall I put up the bed,' he asked.

'I'm too old, I'm too tired and too stressed to lie on the floor,' I said.

MY FIRST SHAMANIC HEALING, that afternoon, was a process of Geoff talking me through a journey that took me to the bottom of the earth. I had tried this in my shamanic meditations but couldn't concentrate enough to fully experience this feeling. Now I felt ready to free my spirit and allow it to travel wherever it needed to go.

'On this journey you may come across your spirit animal,' he said.

'I've tried this at home but I can never relax enough to experience a full shamanic meditation,' I explained. 'Is a spirit animal something that will protect me?'

'In shamanic cosmology everyone has a spirit animal. It's also called a "power animal" or totem,' he explained. 'They're akin to spirit helpers. They don't represent a specific animal but rather the qualities and energy of that species. They're our link to the spirit world, which is why in many traditional cultures people will dance like an animal. Australian Aboriginals may dance like kangaroos or emus, for example. When they do that, they're connecting with the spirit of that animal, channelling it. So, it is a ritual practice. When shamans are connected with their totem, they are in their power.'

As I listened to his soothing voice and the drumming, every muscle in my body relaxed. Thoughts slowly drained from my mind and my anxiety was being drawn out of my side and trickling into a bucket on the floor. The most sublime calm settled — I didn't want this to end.

I pictured the most beautiful bird in the trees filling the winding path down to the depths of the earth. Perched on a branch, with a wide wing span ready to fly, it had a radiant glow around it that captivated me.

After that session I went home, sat down and wrote 2000 words. The words poured out effortlessly. For the first time, I felt at ease with writing about my daily travel stories starting in those early days of settling into our new country. I even found myself laughing out loud at some of my diary entries about the characters on the train on my daily commute.

Overcome with relief and joy, I needed to tell someone who would understand and share in my exhilaration. My email to Geoff was filled with exclamation marks. He responded with praise and encouragement for me to keep going. Like a child, reassurance that I am not lost or losing my mind, is paramount to my recovery. And he did just that.

His method of healing is one of self-examination, inward search and self-healing. It's not mere words but a deeply spiritual healing that flows from his voice, his hands and rituals. Feelings that left me with a curiosity to search for my life's purpose. I believed that everything that happened to me in my life had brought me to him, for a higher purpose.

GEOFF AND I WERE WORKING towards my attendance at a long-standing public speaking event for my book in Wollongong. I was determined to honour the commitment despite a gnawing feeling that I was not ready yet.

The therapy sessions gave me hope but also challenged me. During one session, the confrontation became a turning point. Geoff referred to himself as someone fighting against the spirit of my anxiety. I became acutely aware of the impact this had on my healing particularly while I was in self-sabotage mode.

Many times, during the healing sessions, I experienced a release, a heaviness lifting, rising above me and floating away.

At home I was fighting another battle. Chris, Sasha and Michelin wanted me to try medication and to withdraw from public events. This ring of protection, led to a deeper state of despair.

'You just need to take the edge off,' Sasha said. 'That'll help you calm down.'

'You need to stop working,' Chris added.

'I can't do that,' I'd cry. 'You are asking me to wither away and die.'

'But you're too scared to leave the house. How are you going to get out there?' Michelin threw back at me.

I sought more refuge in the psychology sessions. Geoff worked hard to get me back to living my life the way I'd longed to. Always supportive, encouraging, our sessions also had many light-hearted moments. At the end of one session, he handed me a list of affirmations which I enthusiastically recited during my walks or whenever I was alone. They made me feel more confident and determined to get through this turmoil.

'I must stop trying to control everything,' I said to Geoff. 'That is the hardest thing for me to do. I want to be a good ancestor so that I don't pass this trauma on to other generations in my family.'

'You are definitely too hard on yourself,' he said. 'We all have our own life journey and make our choices, you cannot alter someone's life journey,' he said.

'I read that pain travels through family lines until someone is ready to heal it,' I said. 'That is why I am going through this, this agony of healing so that I won't pass the poison chalice to our generations to come.'

'What about epigenetics?' I asked.

'Some research in epigenetics suggests the effects of trauma might be passed on through generations,' he said.

'I question myself all the time. Why did I fall apart? I come from a long line of strong women. I feel like a failure,' I said.

Before he could answer, I continued to unleash all the thoughts running around in my head.

'When things come together for me, will it fall apart again?' I asked. 'Does the healing allow for this to happen?'

'There is a process for putting things in the past,' he said. 'Sometimes people call me again a few months later because they've relapsed. For some it's a lifelong journey to work on it.'

'I know, but I don't want my struggle to become my identity now. I want to be known as a survivor and not a victim.'

'You think too much,' he said, smiling, maintaining that reassuring eye contact.

WHILE GEOFF AND I had been working towards the presentation, I realised that despite the progress we'd made and even my strong wish for myself to feel confident enough, I wasn't ready. I was shattered. All the work we had been doing seemed in vain. When I received an email from the organisers to inform me that they had 73 people registered and were expecting more over the coming weeks, I decided to keep the news from Geoff. I was terrified of disappointing him. We had even planned a possible early morning healing session to help settle my fears.

So, if this is what I lived for, talking about my book and getting out among the public to share my story and answer their questions, what was I going to be? I was devastated that I seemed to no longer be able to do this.

CHAPTER TEN
QUIET PAIN

The greatest gift you have to give is that of your own self-transformation.

— Lao Tzu

IN MY EAGERNESS to get back to my normal activities, I put enormous pressure on myself. But at home, my crisis was deepening. All everyone talked about was how concerned they were for my welfare. I wanted to scream that I was OK. Sasha had recently qualified as a swimming coach, leaving me on my own most days.

While a calmness had settled for longer periods during the day, panic could be triggered for reasons seemingly unknown.

My mood was, generally, far more upbeat and centred around meditating, writing and cooking or baking. Better concentration led to more focused writing time however the sporadic, often unexplained episodes of panic would throw my day into turmoil. The safest place was inside our home. The only times I ventured out in public were for medical appointments and then I was accompanied by Chris or Sasha. I still struggled to drive and to talk to people on the phone.

Chris, was at his busiest time at work and couldn't just come home whenever I needed him. He called several times a day to check on my wellbeing. This irritated me because most times I had nothing to report. Our conversations were now limited to how I was coping.

'This is not helpful for my recovery.' I lashed out. 'I need everyone to stop tip-toeing around me.'

Keeping quiet about my pain, forever taking care of everyone else's trauma had contributed to this turmoil. I had always been ready to listen to everyone else's problems and offer solutions and support.

Mum and I usually talked on the phone daily, sometimes twice a day. Now I couldn't talk to her longer than a few minutes once a week. I knew Mum understood and put no pressure on me but it troubled me that this was so hard for me to do. I didn't want to worry her with how I felt and what I was going through, and I was thankful she lived a 2-hour drive away because she would have been worried had she seen how I looked.

On our way to therapy one morning, Chris broached the subject of getting a carer for me. Incredulous, I looked at him.

'Are you for real?' I screamed. 'I don't need a carer.'

'Well you cannot stay by yourself during the day and I can't always drop everything and run when you're unable to cope by yourself,' he said

'I'm not getting a carer,' I screamed at him. 'Are you putting me in God's waiting room? You must be out of your mind. I *am* making progress and it won't be long before I'll be out driving again.'

Yet, the familiar muscle twitching, the churning in my stomach had started, and my fear of passing out made me lightheaded. *Just breathe, I willed myself.* We are nearly at therapy.

As soon as the car stopped, I jumped out and headed upstairs. Geoff's door was closed and it meant he either had someone in there or was busy. The blanket on the floor looked like the perfect place to curl up and shut out the world. But I headed to the bathroom where I splashed my face with cold water and stood hunched over the basin. Leaning against the toilet cubicle door, I resorted to my trusted method of calming myself by counting the rows of tiles. My thoughts swirled. *Me get a carer? That's ludicrous. Am I withering away? Will I soon be in a mental institution? Oh God, help me!*

As soon as I spotted Geoff coming out of his office, I stopped outside the entrance to his room.

'I can't go into that room please,' I whispered.

'Is everything OK?' he asked.

'I don't feel like talking,' I said looking at the wall.

In a few moments he had the table setup and I was ready to have my energy restored.

'Do you still pray?' he asked.

'Yes,' I said. 'I pray daily.'

'Close your eyes,' was the last thing I heard Geoff say.

With my head nestled in the soft pillows, I felt my muscles slowly relax. I closed my eyes tight to stop me from looking at the ceiling. I knew the darkness hung there and was waiting to engulf me. Desperate to get away from this pain before Geoff called up the ancestors, I prayed for protection.

'Don't let the darkness win,' I whispered to myself. 'Don't let it win.'

IN THE BACKGROUND, the drums and rattles, the incense and singing bowls and Geoff's chanting filled the room. My thoughts turned to the damaging spin I was on. I had to stop myself from finding offense in anything that my family and others were trying to do to help me. The person I was, happy on the outside and crumbling on the inside, had to go.

Those coping mechanisms that carried me through, needed to go. I wanted to change, to move forward to a different way of living. To be happy and calm on the inside and smiling on the outside. I needed the tools to help me to do it.

Geoff's voice faded into the distance. I had entered into a meditative state, my world of peace and calm, where I walked among the trees and along a glistening lake. I was no longer aware of his usual movements and the sounds of the drums or the singing bowls. During the entire session, my mind relaxed while a healing energy and calm surrounded me. I was receptive and open to this process of healing. My strong belief in his work was the reason I was making progress. During the healing, heat and a mild current spread through my body. I visualised moving images and colours so luminous that my mind felt energised. A deep relaxation spread though my limbs, my neck and face.

I was in no hurry to get up and return to my life outside of this healing room. High anxiety is like being stuck on the shore at low tide. Slowly the water would creep back and sink my feet in the sand. Even with my feet planted down, the sand would bury them, while the earth was still turning and the moon and sun still pulled at the water. My body would fight for more gravity, calmness and peace. *Why am I this way? Can I ever truly love and accept myself?*

'Guess what?' Geoff said. 'I read your book.'

I didn't want to make eye contact. In an instant my past flashed before me. I felt exposed as if a burning light had torn into my flesh Those fears had crept in. Now he will know that my mixed heritage relegated me to second-class citizenship. He'd know those little details of my life that I no longer wanted to discuss, especially with a stranger. This was awkward and embarrassing.

'I must say I was quite naïve about life in South Africa during apartheid,' he continued. 'I didn't pay any attention to what was happening there.'

'I understand,' I mumbled.

Thankfully, when I eventually opened my eyes, he was sitting at his usual spot after a healing. I didn't want to face him and discuss my book.

'I am praying for that day to come when I can wake up and find myself in a place where everything feels right. No racing heart and only positive thoughts. I want to be able to think and see clearly. No dark shadows lurking, waiting to engulf me.

I want to be at peace with my life, everything I've done and achieved and at peace about the future,' I said.

As usual, he nodded and looked at me reassuringly as if to say, 'It's all possible'.

After the healing I felt much calmer than when I arrived. When he mentioned my book, I tried hard to stay positive. As we made our next appointment, we had our usual chat about the week ahead.

'Look at you,' he said. 'You look so Zen. Did you smoke something before coming here?' He laughed.

Now, usually a remark like this would make me laugh, too. It'd be an opportunity to shoot back an appropriate response. However, in my fragile state, I was offended. Had reading my book given him the right to speak to me like this?

'I don't smoke,' I snapped back at him.

Not wanting to lose the energy I had just received, I stormed out. *Am I overreacting? Why couldn't I have a comeback the way I would usually? Have I lost my trademark humour?* I was so touchy about everything. Touchy, that was one of the questions on the weekly Depression, Anxiety and Stress Scale he gave me to complete. I had to tick the 'Everyday' box for touchy.

WHENEVER WE TALKED ABOUT *A Darker Shade of Pale*, memories would flood back about my visit to Cape Town for the launch. I had decided to go to Rhodes Memorial, the scene of my humiliation, where, as a 17-year-old, I'd experienced the brutality of the apartheid regime's *Immorality Act*.

The day the reality of the injustices of the laws of the country stared me in the face. This *Act*, this law, legislated under the apartheid system that was so humiliating and repulsive, ruled that we were only to have relations with our own race.

But on my most recent visit, on top of the mountain of my childhood home town, Oprah Winfrey's words resonated with me.

'When you educate a woman, you set her free. Had I not had books and education in Mississippi, I would have believed that's all there was.'

Proudly I stood on the slopes of the mountain and, much to the surprise of passers-by, screamed, 'This is my book, my book!'.

When I was a 17-year-old on a date, the sounds reverberating were the cries of injustice. Cries, on this very mountain, when police officers enforced the degrading *Immorality Act*. But this time, there was a different echo. The echo of a strong, proud woman inviting the mountain to see what she'd achieved.

I had not set foot on that part of the mountain since. By that day in early 1970s, I had heard about these laws but they did not make any sense and, where I grew up, had no real meaning in my life.

After living in Australia for many years, life had changed. For the past 32 years, I have lived as an ordinary citizen free of the political tangles that so many South Africans are still unravelling.

When we moved to our new homeland, far away from my familiar surroundings, opportunities were abundant. But still, I was the newcomer, the one who had to seek approval and fit in.

Shedding my 'old skin' would prove traumatic. It could mean harsh decisions to deny my ancestors, my heritage or even strip myself of my culture. But there was no chance of that. I would always be asked, 'Where are you from?' People wouldn't want to know if I was a good person or a kind person, but they'd ask the loaded question that spells out its own answer. 'You are an outsider.' *How could I deny my ancestors or my lineage? They endured much worse than I did and survived. Even if it was only just.*

The displacement of my South African culture surfaced, at times, when I least expected it to. I promised myself I'd never leave the town of my birth, my family. I loved my work in our small community in Cape Town — the place where everyone knew my name. Creating development opportunities through music and theatre, in a small way, for the children and young people in our area filled me with a deep sense of purpose. That was my fight against apartheid. If the government would not provide the opportunities for us, in the townships, we'd create them. More often than not, against all odds. And in many ways that would uplift those who had been so badly neglected.

As hard as I tried to see myself as an equal in my new country, my skin was a constant reminder of my past and the insecurity would prove hard to escape. For many in Australia, it was confusing. South Africans were perceived as black or white. I didn't fit that mould. This left me having to explain my lineage and how — under South Africa's laws — my skin shade led to me being classified as coloured. All the enquiries about where I was from were a continual reminder of what I wanted to escape. But there was none. I am an immigrant, a proud one and I'm someone who will always be from another land.

So, in my new society, the need to find my place, drove my need to succeed. Buoyed by the many prospects that fell into my path, every opportunity sent me soaring while I eagerly reaped the recognition. Like a rebirth, a time to expel the stale air and fill my lungs with fresh air, I now had opportunities to exorcise those memories of my stifled development. There were no restrictions now. And the likelihood that I'd fulfil my passion to reach for the stars was greater than ever.

In this process, and in my eagerness to excel, an unstoppable me emerged, a go-getter — work and studies to enhance my skills, motherhood and being a wife, community projects, all melded into someone who set no limits. While juggling a full-time job, like many working mothers, I never missed a school carnival, supervising homework, extra mural activities. I was, as well, the glue that held our extended family together. Added to this was my undying commitment to support charitable projects and individuals in South Africa.

In Australia, when the chances arose to work on some of the country's major events, I jumped at them. I couldn't understand how my colleagues showed little interest in these secondment opportunities to work on events like the Olympics, the Paralympics, and many others. For me, coming from a country where international sanctions isolated us, this was the stuff that dreams were made of.

South Africa's apartheid policies left us deprived of participating in elite level sport. When the international sporting bodies imposed sanctions against South Africa, we missed out on many elite level sporting events. This was not a loss to us because we would not have been able to participate in or attend the majority of these events. Just as there was inequality in education, sport was another contentious issue that divided the nation. Many South Africans were torn between their passion for sport and their commitment to boycotting it as a protest against discriminatory policies. It left many families and communities divided about going to watch international sporting events where only whites could participate. Because of my Dad's vehement opposition to apartheid policies we learned to support international sporting teams.

Now, I didn't want to forego my opportunities to be part of these once-in-a-lifetime events.

Having grown up on the dusty streets of a township, and later, as an adult, living in the same area, there was no escaping oppression. For the majority of South Africa's citizens, life was hampered by the impact of deprivation. Our township had, sadly, become infamous for failure, for raising delinquents or school dropouts. There were scant facilities, and overcrowded conditions. Those who were fortunate to rise above this, did so through sheer determination.

For my siblings and I there were continual reminders from Mum and Dad while growing up — work hard, don't let anyone undermine you. But in South Africa, under apartheid, it was impossible to explore a life equal to those of the oppressors. The moment we stepped outside; they delivered a different message.

'You are not the same as we are.'

I often wondered, when I was growing up, what life was like for the privileged. Thought how good it would be to have white skin and live in a fancy house. I'd become conditioned to the lie that there was a difference between us and them based purely on the colour of our skin.

Once I was in Australia, starry-eyed, my bag brimming with big dreams, and a determination to untangle the shackles of my past, I enthusiastically forged a career. Inspired by the big city lights, tall buildings, tree-lined streets and wide-open spaces, my hopes soared. I could make it here if I worked hard. I was driven by the memory of the many women from my township who worked so hard, in menial jobs, to make a living and provide for their families. Making a good life here was a way to honour them all.

I was determined to also leave a legacy for our future generations; a recognition of where hard work can lead. The thought of it buoyed my spirits. I didn't realise, at the time, that I would lose myself in the process.

It weighed heavily on me that our future generations would look at us as the pioneers who set down roots in Australia. We were starting a new branch of our family in a foreign land and my strong connection to my ancestors spurred me on to leave a legacy to be proud of. When we passed through Australian customs and immigration gates, we were supposed to leave behind the skin that cursed us into a life of oppression. But that was impossible to do. My skin is the essence of who I am. It was an element of my life's journey that I had to come to terms with.

Though devoid of the culture we were born into, like many immigrant families, there was a brighter future for us. There'd be equal and quality education for Sasha and Michelin and future generations. They could pursue any sport they wanted; they had the opportunity to represent Australia if they had the talent and desire. They would grow up free of legislated discrimination and have the opportunities we were denied.

No signs on buildings, benches or public transport or people who'd examine their skin colour or the texture of their hair before they could enter or sit down on a seat. We could buy a house in any area we could afford to, no restrictions. We were free to roam around on any beach. No signs here to instruct us where to sit or stand. It was a strange feeling to enter places and, in particular, train carriages without looking around for others who looked like us.

ON 5 DECEMBER 2013, when news of the death of Nelson Mandela emerged, I hauled out my old manuscript and resumed writing my story.

In 2018, the centenary of Nelson Mandela's life, my life changed forever. Nothing could have prepared me for it. This was the year my long-held dream came true. With it, came a feeling of euphoria that ran so deep, most days it swirled around in the pit of my stomach and filled me with joy.

At the time of my visit to Cape Town, it had been one month since *A Darker Shade of Pale*'s worldwide release. There were many special moments in the lead up to seeing my debut book listed as an Amazon bestseller next to acclaimed and respected writers I deeply admired. The excitement of my first publishing contract, the first glimpse of my book cover, the layout of my book, and even the look of the font consumed my waking moments. (I won't lie, many times still, I've felt the urge to whip out a copy of my book and show it to the stranger sitting next to me. Of course, I stopped myself.)

My writing journey had not been easy. It was fraught with fallen rocks and winding paths leading to nowhere. After many years of starting and stopping, the task had seemed impossible.

It started with a fantasy in an ill-equipped, township high school on the Cape Flats of South Africa. I was living among the sand dunes and blocks of concrete flats in council housing estates. The setting reeked of deprivation and failure. But among the dusty roads and overcrowded houses, rose many pillars of strength. Parents who grappled with hardship through menial jobs were the drivers of our path. They prepared us for a better future.

And now, standing at Rhodes Memorial, near the spot where I was vilified as a young woman, I thought of the thousands of other people who experienced my pain and humiliation. As a citizen in South Africa I knew no life other than that of injustice and inequality. I could aspire to be like those who revelled in a privileged classification. But achieving it was impossible; in the eyes of the law my skin was too dark. I was born with mixed heritage, at the wrong time, on South African soil, one of many enduring the abuse of our human rights.

When I looked across the slopes at the vast landscape, I felt at peace with having grown up in this unequal society. I lived an ordinary life in a country going through an extraordinary time in its history. Now, my footsteps, once forbidden in these surrounding suburbs, were welcomed everywhere.

AS I DRANK IN MY LAUNCH MOMENT, it was more than the excitement of my book launches, the praise and admiration, that filled me.

I prayed that somewhere in this, my birth town, a girl who looked like me, with a dream like I had, would overcome her fear and pick up a pen and write. Not just write, but follow her dreams, even achieve them much sooner than I had. I hoped that she, in turn, would lead others to write their stories.

My achievement is also dedicated to the young girls and boys, to women and men who have dreams and those who need encouragement to fulfill them. As they run towards those dreams, I hope that courage will stem their fears and the words in their souls will find a way onto the pages of their books. I know fear, it has gripped me for most of my life, but when that moment arrives where fear gives way to a greater purpose, then they must be ready.

I was overcome by the realisation that my mother's steadfast belief in education and the power it had, despite all we faced, to save us. She had extraordinary foresight in that overcrowded environment and, rather than any despair overwhelming her, her belief spurred her on. She tackled the long road on her bicycle every morning to her job in the bakery. She had her plan for our future and devoted her life to fulfilling it. She felt no greater joy than to see us dressed for school with satchels filled with books and pens. Our report cards and book prizes were her reward.

For a few moments I turned my face to the mountain and wept. My dream realised was also her dream fulfilled.

IN OUR TOWNSHIP there was a small library. It was our source of entertainment, and opened our world to life in other parts of the universe. It was there that I escaped to and read the books that made me dream about writing my own adventures.

Whether it's writing a book, or baking a special cake, or buying your first home, making your dream come true is like dancing with wildness on a mountain to a song in your head. And, how can I forget that exhilarating feeling in the tips of my fingers when I typed *The End* on my manuscript.

On the mountain I saluted the many fallen souls who fought that brutal regime to bring freedom in South Africa.

Our history, our stories must continue to be heard. These memories encouraged me, made me feel my worth.

CHAPTER ELEVEN
BRINK OF DESPAIR

Fear cannot be banished, but it can be calm and without panic; it can be mitigated by reason and evaluation.

—Vannevar Bush

MY WRITING DESK, always offered an escape when sleep evaded me. I'd spend hours researching my writing projects or checking on emails. Through my events and since writing the book I had many emails to respond to, only now I didn't have the inclination to reply. There were several invitations to speaking events from schools and community groups that remained unanswered.

In the early hours, on a sleepless night, an email from the book distributor in Cape Town caught my attention.

'Have a look at our page. We don't want you to reply but just to be aware about the comments in response to our promotion of your book,' it said.

Below their post a discussion had ensued about my intelligence and my limited knowledge about the current situation in South Africa. The remarks were personal and inflammatory about my being someone living outside of South Africa. The comments about my lineage and lack of credibility as a writer were deeply hurtful.

'Books like this is [sic] responsible for the current white genocide,' someone wrote.

I started clicking on unopened messages in my inbox.

In the dark of night, I wanted the right to defend myself. *'Why don't they read my book?'* I muttered to myself. Instead of shutting down social media, I started reading. The more I read, the more restless and angrier I became. So I took myself to my other room, and tried to settle into meditation in the dark. There was no one to talk to at that hour.

I knew that if I told Chris he'd be furious, curse and then, insist I take a break from all my activities. That was not the solution. I couldn't hide from the world forever. I had to find that switch that was the positive, strong me and flick it back on. It was not in my character to crumble in defeat.

I emailed Geoff to show him what people were saying about me. I needed an outlet, someone to listen and understand.

GEOFF CALLED THE NEXT DAY to talk about my reactions, my despair, and offered some practical tips to protect myself. 'We'll discuss this more in-depth at your appointment in a couple of days but in the meantime get someone else to check your emails and let others know that they're not to alert you about these vile messages,' he said.

The next day, to Chris's relief, I decided to pull out of the speaking engagement in Wollongong. The thought of facing a large crowd terrified me. I realised then how much work I still had to do.

In the meantime, my thoughts had become more and more consumed with past trauma. I recalled a workplace harassment, a stalker, online and schoolyard bullying, losing my siblings and the decision to end my career prematurely. All of the memories rocked my sense of self-worth. I sank to a new low.

Three months of weekly sessions had passed and I expressed my frustration about my slow progress. I was also regularly beginning to think about trying medication. Slowly, defeat was creeping in. My sleeping pattern was still erratic. Some nights I was scared to sleep because waking up in the nightmare was hell.

Sensing my vulnerability and hesitation about medication, Geoff offered a solution.

'If you feel so strongly about not using medication, then set yourself a target of four weeks from now. If nothing changes then speak to your doctor.'

Geoff's suggestion was sound, gave me comfort and made me more determined to try harder to overcome my fears and improve my mood. I'd ventured out to the shops with Sasha and managed to spend two hours shopping. That was progress. Sasha and I had a pamper session and I managed to get through it — even if it was necessary to listen to a meditation throughout the pampering. That was progress. I had taken short drives by myself to the physiotherapist. That was progress. But I was eager for more independence.

'I miss people,' I told Geoff. 'I want to go out to dinner with family and friends and talk about stuff and laugh and…'

He nodded. 'Soon,' he said, smiling and reassuring me, 'you will'.

'I'm so impatient, I want to feel myself again.'

'I can see you're still really struggling with these traumas. You are not responding quite the way we'd like, are you?' he continued.

'Yes, I do feel that my recovery is slow,' I said.

'OK, that's why I want to do some more intensive exposure work,' Geoff said. 'It involves what we call imagery rescripting, which is very common for trauma.'

'You know I'm prepared to do whatever it takes,' I said looking at him directly, I wanted him to feel my eagerness to do this work.

'Well, trauma treatments generally expose people to their traumatic memories. In my shamanic work I also use trance work for trauma.'

'Will I go into a trance?'

'Yes, hypnosis is trance work. But we move in and out of

different states of consciousness throughout the day. When you meditate you shift consciousness. When you hear my drum, you shift too.'

'Are you going to use the drum?'

'No,' he laughed. 'For you we'll do it using hypnotherapy.'

'Hypnotherapy?'

'Not the sort of hypnotherapy you see on TV,' he smiled. 'But for now, let me show you what I mean.'

My regular practice of meditation made it easier for me to relax while I waited for his instructions. My eyelids gently closed, eyeballs were still and centred which allowed my breathing to slow down. Soon his soothing voice took me on a journey to a place I visualised, filled with beauty and a deep tranquillity. I waited for the feeling of losing control but all I felt was peace and calmness.

'NOW SLOWLY BRING YOURSELF back and open your eyes,' he said.

When I opened my eyes, Geoff, understanding what I needed, said, 'You will be in complete control of your mind at all times.'

'How soon can we start this therapy?' I asked.

'In a week or so,' he said. 'In the meantime, you should increase your meditation to 45-minute sessions.'

'I'm struggling to keep my mind from wandering after even twenty minutes,' I laughed.

'It's important to lengthen the sessions, much like a doctor increasing your dosage of medication,' he said and handed me a Christian meditation book.

'Have a read and try and use some of the chanting it mentions. It should help you focus during your meditation.'

That week, I increased my walking program, and successfully started practising 45-minute meditations. I also engaged more with people on the phone.

For years, I wished I could figure out how to address my

anxieties so the cycle of response and panic would be easier to break. Meditation had become one of the practices I could do whenever anxious thoughts disrupted the calm. I'd become adept at calming myself with a breathing practice and by using a mantra from the Christian meditation book. The mantra, 'Ma-ra-na-tha' meant 'Come Lord Jesus Come'. It cleared my mind and brought me back to the moment though it worked only if I could recite the mantra before my anxieties took hold. Once racing thoughts took off, it was a struggle to calm myself. Daily walks were able to distract me, but it was easier to lose motivation doing only the walking.

When my close friend Tracy suggested she pick me up for a drive to the beach and lunch, I agreed, nervously. Tracy's calm and deep religious beliefs made it easy for me to be in her company. Yet, as the day of our date grew closer, my fears intensified. I hadn't been out of the house for a social engagement for several months, neither had I engaged with anyone other than medical professionals or my family. I started searching for reasons not to go.

Even though Tracy regularly sent me uplifting music and scripture passages to encourage me, when she pulled into the driveway in her yellow convertible Mustang, I froze. I started convincing myself that I'd suffer a panic attack and she wouldn't know what to do.

She came inside, sat across from me in the lounge and chatted about the weather and where we should go for our drive. I struggled to remain calm. My out-of-control feeling angered me and before leaving home I retreated to the bathroom, where I counted tiles.

When Tracy and I left the house, my jittery feelings continued. I tried to ignore the signals to squirm in my seat. Soon, as we were driving along the beachfront, I breathed a bit more easily. This was a welcome break from the four walls at home. When we stopped to eat our take-away lunch we were facing the beach. My legs were trembling. I knew the signs. So I slowed my breathing. Any rapid breathing would lead to a panic attack and all my muscles would tighten. If Tracy noticed my unease, she didn't show it. Happily, she chatted and played music.

Softly, I started chanting to myself — a word from the meditation book. Looking at the vast ocean helped calm any racing thoughts and I decided to venture out of the car.

I tried to open the door. But my fear wouldn't allow it. I sat still, longing to walk in the water and allow the ocean to wash away my fears, but I felt safer inside the car. Tracy got out and went to the back of her car. She began looking for something, though I don't know what. I plugged in my earphones to listen to my meditation. My face started relaxing, my breathing slowed but the trembling continued.

'Can we drive please?'. I turned to ask Tracy who'd climbed back into her driver's seat. 'I need to be on the move.'

Without questioning my urgency, she started driving and we cruised around the streets of Cronulla until it was time to surprise Chelsea and Charlotte with a ride home in the Mustang.

These felt like small steps, but I was making progress.

At my weekly visit with Carlo, he had suggested I download a binaural beats app to play through my headphones to help me cope with these extreme anxious periods. My fear of falling in public was one of the scariest.

'I use these binaural beats daily,' he said. 'Let's build a survival kit for you. Get some essential oils like lavender, keep the binaural beats and daily meditation on your phone. Use them when you feel disaster is about to strike. I am on the other end of the phone if BPPV happens and I, or someone at the clinic, will always be able to help you.'

My first episode of BPPV a few years earlier had me wide awake at 3.00 am with the room spinning rapidly. I couldn't lift my head and screamed at Chris to call an ambulance. I had no idea what was happening. When the paramedics arrived, they got me out of bed but all I felt was that I was riding a huge wave in rough seas. I was vomiting and the paramedics walked me to a corner so I could feel the walls next to me. They administered anti-nausea medication and then took me to hospital. Though I was still unable to walk without the room spinning, I was discharged the next day to go home and rest.

After two years of frustration with not getting solutions to my health problems, I now had supportive practitioners to help me heal physically, mentally and spiritually and they made a huge difference to my self-confidence. I was determined to be well again.

CHAPTER TWELVE
NEXT-LEVEL THERAPY

There is no greater agony than bearing an untold story inside you.

— Maya Angelou

MY WEEKLY THERAPY SESSIONS with Geoff brought mixed results. In some sessions, I felt confident I was making progress. In other sessions my inability to let him into my darkest fears held me back. My recurring dreams continued to affect my sleep and I was still terrified of leaving home on my own or socialising.

Whenever I achieved some success in leaving the house or driving myself somewhere without turning back, I'd give myself a mental pat on the back and send Geoff an email to report my progress. This interaction with him was vital to my recovery. I needed reassurance that I was sane and this was only a hitch and not a death sentence.

There were also some moments where Geoff would confront my negativity and they had an adverse effect on my relationship with him as a practitioner. I saw his reaction as critical of me and not as him trying to help me. My therapeutic relationship with him fluctuated. Whenever I had to confront my trauma, I viewed him differently. His physical appearance reminded me of my oppressors yet around him, as an aura, was a different light, a sense that my spirit was welcomed.

After one particularly calming energy healing session, I felt a sudden urge to go to church. As a practising Catholic, I had always seen Sunday Holy Mass as an important and solemn obligation.

'I haven't been to church in several months,' I said.

'Oh, really?' he said. 'Maybe you should go if you feel so strongly about it.'

'I was in hospital on Christmas eve so I missed Midnight Mass for the first time in my life,' I replied. 'I've tried to get to church several times, but I know I can't sit long enough. I get too anxious. I just can't … and I don't know how to fix it.'

'I don't want any negativity when we're doing this work.' He sounded stern and his expression changed. His jaw had tightened, gone was the friendly face. His tone sent a clear message. I had to make decisions about what I wanted. Immediately, I regretted opening up to him about this fear. My unease resurfaced and I got more and more defensive. *Can he really help me? Am I putting too much faith in him?*

At the same time, though, the encounter forced me to make a choice about moving to the next level in my therapy. It jolted me into a determination to erase the negative thoughts.

A week later I ventured on my first solo drive in many months and decided to drive myself to my therapy session. The 20-minute drive to Sutherland, in traffic, was daunting. As usual, my brain came up with terrifying images. But now I had some coping mechanisms. My regular panic might involve having left the stove on and visualising firefighters dousing our house to try and save it, or vivid images of our dog, Marley, being bitten by a snake in the backyard.

Now, I had the tools to banish these scenarios from my mind.

Throughout the drive I wrestled with myself. At times, I focused on self-talk, reciting affirmations to keep my attention on the road. At times a level of weakness and fear crept in. I switched between positive self-talk and a disciplining tone, and wildly fearful scenarios. But I immediately followed those with reassurances that I could keep calm. Other drivers on the road must have been intrigued by this woman animatedly talking to herself!

Chris had called before I left home and once during the drive and hearing him encouraged me. I successfully made the 20-minute drive.

With adrenaline cascading through my limbs, I burst through the door at therapy. I was so relieved that I dropped my car keys and handbag, and spontaneously hugged Geoff. My spirit was soaring, but I also needed a drink to calm my nerves.

Geoff, with his trademark smile and kind eyes embraced me and my exuberance. He clearly recognised my achievement. It was one of the highlights of our work to date.

My determination and success in getting from home to therapy was a tremendous confidence boost. After three months of therapy, this was the breakthrough I needed since progressively losing my confidence over the past 12 months. Independence beckoned. And in my eyes was a glimmer of hope, dancing.

THAT THERAPY SESSION WAS DIFFERENT. The darkness that usually lurked in the shadows or popped out at me from the bookshelf was nowhere to be seen. We spoke in-depth about my fears. Geoff, always generous, filled the room with so much light. His relaxed demeanour; and his enthusiasm lifted my spirits to a new level. I felt inspired about the work we were about to do. But, all too soon the session seemed to end and we still had so much more to unravel. The session had ended with Geoff channelling a calming, healing energy and a pact that I wouldn't let those who are causing me such grief win.

'I won't let them win,' were my parting words.

And then, there was the drive home. It was a breeze. No self-talk was needed.

'She's back,' wrote Sasha in a text message.

'Way to go, Mum,' said Michelin's message.

Armed with some new coping mechanisms and Geoff's promise that my therapy would move to the next level, I had fresh hope.

MY EAGERNESS TO START this new therapy couldn't have prepared me for the pain that lay ahead.

How could I explore the traumatic experiences in my life? How would I articulate everyday racial vilification for the first 30 years of my life? There were so many incidences. Many massive, some seemingly slight. All were triggers, even if I no longer lived with them daily.

In writing *A Darker Shade of Pale*, I'd unearthed a deep-rooted anger about how we were forced to live. I had contempt for those who oppressed us. That they'd lived with the power over us for as long as they did frustrated me to the point of hatred. Wealth and privilege by dint of skin colour was utterly unacceptable. Memories — of deep cuts and others more fleeting, flooded back — of colleagues sitting in cafés while I was refused entry; racist comments from brainwashed colleagues, especially one who said that marrying someone from a coloured race group would tarnish his bloodline. A confrontation with a high school bully, when I was 15, which made me want to run away from home. The death of my father, the hopelessness of my brother George's early death, watching Frances suffer for an extended period before she died; the tragedy and guilt of Owen's drowning, the gruesome deaths of childhood friends. The humiliating experience of Michelin, as a two-year-old being refused a bed in a hospital ward because of his skin colour. Being harassed and stalked at work in Australia, and my forced decision to retire. Searing too, were the times I unearthed racist attitudes in my adopted country that matched those from South Africa.

I'd seen many dire things in my lifetime, people depleted of hope. There is nothing worse than an amputated spirit. There's no prosthetic for that.

How would I get closure when the very issues I seek closure from are the issues that shaped who I am. This was definitely not going to be easy. But I wanted to confront them all.

I HAD GROWN TO TRUST Geoff implicitly. In that therapy room, he saw me in my brokenness, at my most vulnerable. On many occasions, he had lifted me out of the depths of despair. This new therapy, I thought, was going to be no different to what we had been doing.

Despite my fear, part of me knew it was time to forgive myself for all the things I did not achieve. I had accomplished enough. Because of my tough start in life I'd had a raging need to fix things for others so they would not experience hardship.

It was time to stop worrying about others being disappointed that I wasn't the inspiring person they thought I was.

I realised that with my drive of wanting to achieve, I didn't know how to be like other people, who were content with living their lives differently to the way I lived mine. With me it was either everything or nothing. On the days when I wasn't everything, I considered myself weak, vulnerable and broken.

It was time to accept that I couldn't save everyone. Time to be thankful for what I'd accomplished in helping others.

Things had shifted. I no longer had to prove I was successful by being a high functioning person. Doing less did not mean I'd lost my power, it only meant I had a new focus. I desperately needed rest from the character that I'd been playing for so long.

THAT WEEK, BEFORE THE EXPOSURE, my nervous system remained on high alert. I wrestled between daily panic attacks that left me curled up in bed for extended periods of time and pushing myself to go out for a walk, and to meditate.

In my solitude, I could no longer pretend everything was OK. My ritual of meditation and prayers kept me calm and focused.

This was followed by long periods of silence, on our back deck, or sitting at my desk where I'd lose myself in the words pouring out of my soul.

The week before the start of my much-anticipated new therapy, I had another breakthrough. I went on an unplanned two-hour shopping spree with Sasha. Relaxed and in control of my emotions I walked around the shopping centre, sat down for coffee, laughed and chatted like everyone else around me. Throughout the afternoon, I practised self-talk strategies. Out loud, I said to myself, for what seemed like, a thousand times: 'Stop worrying. You are safe. If something bad was to happen, Sasha is right here and will get you safely back to the car'.

As if by divine intervention, my fear sensors had disappeared. No anxiety. Nothing. I sensed that I belonged in the world.

Then, towards the two-hour mark, I started feeling jitters in my limbs. I'd spotted a couple who usually attended my events and wanted to avoid having to talk to them. The churning in the pit of my stomach took hold. I needed the safety of the car.

'Are you still OK to walk around?' asked Sasha. 'You've gone quiet.'

'Give me the keys,' I mumbled. 'I need air.'

'There is no air in the carpark,' she laughed. 'Come, let's go together. You've done it, Mum, you should send a message to your psychologist,' she laughed. 'You are cured!'

Cured? I was far from it. Suddenly, again, being anxious felt logical, the only way my nervous system could cope. Prolonged anxiety and trauma were trapped in my cell memory. No matter how hard I tried again, to calm down using Geoff's strategies of self-talk and positive thoughts, the worst scenarios slipped back into my head.

But I was, still, able to recover some balance. 'When I say I'm always sad,' I said to Sasha, and also to myself, 'it doesn't mean that I'm never happy,' I said. 'It just means there's always some level of anxiety there.'

As I spoke to her, I remembered a conversation I'd had with Geoff.

'I have to fight that wave of hopelessness and confusion that can surface without warning,' I said.

'Remind yourself of the goodness around you,' Geoff said, often. 'Practise gratitude, imagine the typical safety of the world around you.'

'Good things don't cancel out the horrible things,' I said. 'I can't show gratitude and not feel anything about the horrible things.'

In continued therapy sessions I was encouraged to divulge more of my fears and traumatic memories. Talking to Geoff helped to validate my fears that it was OK not to be OK. In that small room, more often, I found the courage to pull myself back up and carry on living. Sitting, or sometimes because of my anxiety, standing, in the therapy room while I expressed my fears, I let go of a lot of shame. I allowed it to die right there in that room.

SOMETIMES, HOWEVER, VIGILANCE was the safest route for me. Breaking the anxiety proved harder than I ever imagined. I needed more than positive thoughts to get me through episodes when I spiralled out of control. I understood that my personality came from the habits and behaviours I'd developed because of anxiety. My personality had helped me to cope.

During dark moments, I'd jot down my thoughts in an email to Geoff to let him know the battle raging inside of me. It usually helped me to fall back to sleep once I had sent the message. There would always be an encouraging reply.

'You've taught me about self-talk and talking to my anxiety, being brutal in confronting it,' I'd remind him. 'But… I don't like this crying.'

'Crying doesn't indicate that you're weak. It's really been an indication you're alive. This room does, that.' He smiled. 'Don't be afraid to let the tears flow if you need to.'

'This thing with putting things in the past is exhausting,' I said. 'I know my past mistakes have got me to where I am today but it's hard to change my way of thinking.'

'No matter how long you've travelled in the wrong direction, you can always turn around. Learn to forgive yourself,' he said gently.

'I know you're helping me free my mind but I have to walk through that open door on my own,' I said. 'That's the scary bit. There's loads of guilt and shame and heartache cause I feel I no longer belong. I forget to be gentle with myself and love me for who I am — perfectly imperfect.'

'Try nurturing your body and soul with healing foods, thoughts and nature. And remember that no matter what, you are enough,' he said.

'I want to be like everyone else around me,' I said. 'What about others you've treated? Are there different levels of anxiety?'

'Well there's normal anxiety which everyone has, there is what we call 'sub-clinical' anxiety — its high and can be somewhat problematic but not bad enough to significantly impair the way you function in daily life,' he explained. 'Then there are 'clinical' levels of anxiety, where the anxiety is interfering with functionality. Anxiety is a continuum from normal which everyone has, to extreme distress.'

'I know we've worked on a few strategies over these months. I know confronting my anxiety has been key,' I said.

'Oh yes,' he said. 'Exposure is a key part of my treatment. The only way to get over anxiety properly,' he went on to explain, 'is to face what your mind is telling you is dangerous. That exposure is done gently and slowly. He paused. 'And it's done in a hierarchical way.'

'Let's say, for example, if a person is anxious of spiders, then the exposure would begin with them looking at a picture of a cartoon spider, then have them look at a real spider web, then looking at a real spider. It doesn't have to be abrupt exposure to the feared situation.'

And so, as time progressed, with a lot of self-work, insight, and just plain irritation with this unsettling pattern, I found ways to start managing my fears. At times, redirecting the negative thoughts became easier. I started feeling I'd completely moved on in some areas; that the freak of a person who had taken over my life for such a long time was slowing fading.

CHAPTER THIRTEEN
TRAUMA, MY BROKEN SPIRIT

Nothing good comes without trial.

— Dr Geoff Lyons

THE DAY I'D BEEN WAITING FOR— the start of my first hypnotherapy session — finally arrived. With it, and despite a general sense of optimism, negative thoughts intermittently swirled in my mind. *What if this doesn't work? Will I be in therapy forever?*

Inside the therapy room Geoff's demeanour was professional and focused. His jaw was clenched, he avoided my eyes as he rustled through the papers on a small table next to his chair. The silence was unbearable. I needed to babble to lighten the atmosphere. I had become used to his friendly and welcoming manner. Now the room had a clinical feel.

I glanced at his face, searching for any indication of what to expect from this session. No sign. My eye spotted a small recorder next to his papers.

'Are you recording this?' I asked.

'Yes,' he replied. 'Imagery work is often recorded.'

Hypervigilance kicked in. *Why must he record this? Is this a case study? Do I really want anyone else to listen to my mental health issues?*

'If you are not comfortable then I won't record it,' he suggested. 'But it can be good for you to have a copy of the session. That way you can practice exposure at home.'

We settled on what would be recorded and then he offered

me his seat. He definitely wasn't his usual funny self. I tried to get into the zone as well to match his professionalism.

'Now, we will explore memories that could be hard. But remember, you are in complete control. If you want to stop at any time, open your eyes and we'll stop,' he said.

Then I heard him say, 'Now, just like we did the other day, I want you to take a deep breath in, exhale slowly, take another deep breath in, exhale slowly'.

I allowed my eyes to gently close, my eyeballs relaxed and my eyelids resting gently. My hands clasped, lay in my lap. For once my legs did not tremble. All I could hear was my breathing. The anticipation, the silence, my shallow breathing, cheeks and jaw relaxed. Pure bliss.

Moments later, Geoff's voice carried me on a journey. Powerful words filled the recesses of my mind. From deep within my soul, his words lulled me into a hypnotic state. Floating on a soft cloud one moment, clear fresh air permeated my lungs. His words guided me through calm and beautiful landscapes.

Every word filled my senses, cradled my broken spirit, rocking it gently before lifting it out of the dark. I felt a renewed strength surge through my body. The most awe-inspiring feeling emerged as we walked through time and space. I felt a sense of empowerment and freedom.

Spellbound by the richness of the images in my surroundings, with no sense of time and place, my soul soared into the spheres. I remained glued to my seat, afraid to move my head, for fear of losing concentration, I followed the pathways into the unknown. I wanted to store these moments in my vault in readiness for when the darkness crushed me. I captured as many as I could.

But, as I travelled into my childhood, the protective cordon shattered. Fear crept in. Attempts to shake it off only heightened my senses. My childhood memories had me squirming. *Concentrate.* My stomach was churning as nausea pushed its way up my oesophagus, curdling, choking its way out. *Keep floating on that cloud. Breathe,* I willed myself. *Take control.* This is the moment we've been working towards. Seize it. But there was no stopping the pressure.

'Now slowly open your eyes,' I heard Geoff say.

His voice was encouraging, gentle, inviting me back into the setting. But too late. Nausea filled my system. Rushing out of the room to the bathroom, the pressure exploded. Anxious that my reaction may have jeopardised the work, I fretted when I got home.

The recording, though, gave me a renewed hope, inspired me to stay positive and continue the therapy. Daily, sometimes several times, I heard Geoff's words and the reminder of the magical journey released my inner turmoil. A radiant light shone around me.

After that shaky start, Geoff continued to assure me that our work held promise. That week, my daily ritual of walking, praying, meditating, and affirmations now included listening to the recording. My toolkit had an added element. With my renewed sense of strength, I had glimpses of my adventurous personality. Going out on my own to the shops and other public places was now at the top of my list but it still eluded me.

The next therapy session explored harder traumatic memories in my life, and it frightened me. This time, however, the setting was different: his speech intense, the words sharp and targeted. Moving through the trauma that had embedded itself so deeply in my memory, my legs started hurting. Squirming around in the chair, I picked up every sound in the room, the rustling of his papers, and the tone of his voice.

But Geoff encouraged me to look at memories that I didn't want to visit. As we worked through my trauma, my fears raged. At times it felt surreal. The sensations, smells, sounds, and voices of my past started to overwhelm me.

'Remember the power animals? Be in your power,' Geoff instructed. 'You are not a child. Be strong.'

The intensity in Geoff's voice brought a surge of adrenaline. My 15-year-old self, raw and hurting, proved the toughest to conquer. But I was cooperating with his instructions and we powered through the memory. The vision of my old self, crumbled, when the taunts rang in my ears. My resistance faltered, crushed, my heart broke. Victimhood had set in. I buried my face in my hands as a flood of sobs racked my body.

'You are not that child; you are powerful just like your ancestors. Find your power and go back,' Geoff urged.

Wrenching myself back into the moment, I continued to confront these traumatic memories head on. At times, I was functioning outside of my body, attacking the trauma with every ounce of my being, before pain overwhelmed me. Geoff's voice, always encouraging, spurring me on to dig deep into the trenches and go to war.

Towards the end of the session, mentally drained, and on high alert, I was exhausted. Onward we ploughed, brutally confronting these traumatic memories. Many times, throughout the session, Geoff's voice pulled me back to the moment. He offered to stop. **But I didn't want to.**

UTTERLY DRAINED BUT STILL ON A HIGH, I fell into a deep sleep that night. My first dreamless sleep in many years.

The next morning, raring to go, I went for a walk. I clocked up my first 6-kilometre walk. Then, disaster struck. As I walked past a group of workmen, a piece of metal lodged in my eye. I got myself home and Chris rushed me to the Sydney eye hospital for emergency treatment. I had sustained a severe eye trauma including lacerations across my cornea. I panicked as I couldn't see clearly out of my left eye. My resistance to my fears crumbled. I spent the night at the hospital worried that I'd lose the sight in my eye.

As the pain medication began working, the darkness slowly rolled in and hung in my sightline ready to engulf me. While I don't remember much of the message, I had sent Geoff, his reply gave me instructions how to calm myself and practice self-healing. My reply was that the world was against me. These accidents and incidents had happened most of my life. All the bad memories surfaced and, blinded by self-pity, I plunged into the black hole.

'Don't worry too much,' Geoff's message read. 'We'll fix it at our next session.'

But my mood was dark. I was filled with rage and refused to cooperate. All my hard work was in vain.

'No one can help me, not you, not God,' I shot back. 'This is my punishment for all my failings.'

As I lay in the hospital bed, tears streamed down. I listened to the sounds in the room and though I was exhausted, I was afraid of the nightmare hell that awaited, I thought of how comforting it would be to have my eye specialist, the late Dr Evan Soicher, treat me. This made me think of death. And, my thoughts turned to how peaceful death would be.

'Come and see me when you're home,' Geoff offered. 'We'll work through this.'

After I recovered for three days with drops to slow down my eye movements, and antibiotics to clear infection, Chris drove me to therapy.

My latest speaking event was two weeks away and the excitement had just started building. I had a renewed determination to work harder in therapy. I wasn't afraid to leave home.

It was important for me to go out and talk about my writing journey, my story. These events remained my lifeline for rediscovering myself and rebuilding my passion for the things I felt so strongly about.

With bloodshot eyes, highly anxious, I arrived at therapy. Geoff looked at me sympathetically for a few moments before changing his tack.

'I suggest we go back into battle with your trauma,' he said.

Is he for real? Can't he see I've just suffered an eye trauma and I'm in no state to go into battle?

'I don't think I can,' I said avoiding his eyes. 'I've just been knocked down; my wings are broken. Can't you see?'

'Your eye accident happened less than 24 hours after our last session and that would have affected all the work we did,' he explained. 'We should try and change that now so that this treatment remains effective.'

'I can't,' I insisted.

'What is going on here is hard,' he said. 'But you must continue the work otherwise you will be back where you started.'

'At this very moment, I don't care about anything,' I shot back. 'Can't you see that I am doomed? This happens to me all the time. I've had enough of all this trauma.'

Moving forward in his chair, he stared at me intently. Trying to avert his gaze, I looked at the bookshelf but quickly turned away. My eyes rested on the titles.

I had sunk into the state I was before starting therapy. Once again, I allowed anxiety to take control. I had to fight, tell myself to stand up straight, stop rocking or squirming in my seat, stop shaking, just breathe, calm down. I had to take control.

My silence, confusing at times for others, meant that I was wrestling with my anxiety. I don't handle conflict very well; my resistance goes up several notches while I process the perceived danger. At that moment, I couldn't talk to Geoff until I had settled my thoughts. But he pushed on.

'I have a duty to ask you this. Are you suicidal?'.

That questioned rocked my world.

'No,' I shot back. 'What kind of question is that?' I asked. 'Even if I was, I would not tell you.'

'Come get up,' he urged. 'Let's summon your power.'

Reluctantly, I got up to face him. Through my blurred vision, the room no longer held that safe feeling. It looked smaller and darker; more threatening than I had ever felt in it. I needed the sacred space in the bigger room where my energy is usually restored.

'Stand up,' he encouraged.

Without waiting for me to respond, he called out affirmations.

'I am powerful,' he shouted.

'No! I am weak,' I said.

'OK, I don't think we should continue,' he said. 'I think you should go.'

'Why?' I shouted. 'Can't we do something else. Can't you see I am injured?'

In silence he picked up his papers and a stony expression had spread over his face. His jaw clenched; and, for a few moments, cold eyes glared at me. He was dark and angry, and his eyes no longer held comfort. He used his eyes to motion for me to leave through the open door. A strong message to get out. *Why is he being so mean? This is so unfair.*

If I leave now, under these conditions, then there will be no return and all our work would have been in vain. *What will I tell my family?* They've all been so happy with my progress over these last few weeks. Reaching for my bag, wrestling with my pride and emotions, I hesitated.

Geoff seized the moment and pounced on my vulnerability and confusion.

'I am fighting against the spirit of your anxiety right now,' he exclaimed. The tone of his voice was different, it grew louder, as if he wanted to get inside my head. 'This is what happens when I treat people who suffer with various addictions as well,' he said, his eyes remained fixed on mine. 'I end up fighting the spirit of their addictions. But ... but you need to fight it harder than me. Your victory must come from you!'

The tone in his voice startled me. In an instant, memories of my past oppression triggered. It felt as if I was standing face-to-face with a white, oppressive bully, ordering me to have my tea downstairs with the other coloureds. My defences were on high alert. Images flashed of being trapped in an office, as a young woman in apartheid South Africa, facing my employer. At that time, I was the only coloured person working in an office under an oppressive, arrogant white bully and he was chastising me. I felt rage curse through my arms, in readiness to lash out at Geoff. I had to defend myself against his harshness; his oppressive behaviour.

My nervous system, in overdrive, was tricking me into thinking trauma was happening right now. Geoff's lips were moving; his hands were suspended in the air explaining psychological concepts. But I could not focus. My eyes were tearing. I needed my eyedrops to stop the burning sensation.

Concentrate.

But he had sensed my wavering. This was the moment, to get me out of this dissociative state. Holding my attention, he brought me back to the present and out of those crushing traumatic thoughts that had engulfed me. We were now in a brutal battle — me in the 'spirit of my anxiety' and him, against the spirit of my anxiety.

Standing across from him, recognising how much he wanted to help me, I dropped my bag and quietly stood up straight to do the affirmations. Rushing to shut the door, Geoff sprang into action, shouting out affirmations and gathering his papers. Conscious of the urgency to get me back in the chair, he revved up the volume until our voices joined in unison. *I am powerful. I am strong. I am brave.*

Back in the chair I felt a new power surge through my arms and legs. My mind, however, dreaded what was coming – the painful process of attacking my trauma.

'Breathe in, centre yourself,' Geoff instructed. 'Everything's okay.'

With the same gentleness that I had grown used to he settled my racing mind. Soon I was in a calm hypnotic state. Taking me through the traumatic memories that I had recorded in my memoir, Geoff continued to dig beneath the layers that *A Darker Shade of Pale* had unearthed. As I returned to the family trauma surrounding my sister Frances's death, my body revolted. I was wracked by the family rift, my guilt and how much I needed to grieve her. I missed her so terribly and longed to hear her voice, her cursing, our political and sporting debates and mostly her crazy laughter. So much journeying through life together. Whenever Geoff and I spoke about her death, the focus remained on the family rift and talk about her being gone was pushed into the background.

At that moment, I longed for things to return to normal. My muscles tensed, and my body started shaking. A chill had crept into my bones.

'I'm cold,' I whispered.

'I'll turn off the air-conditioner,' he said. 'We are nearly finished, just a little bit longer and then this will be over.'

But I could not stop shaking. The chill in my body made it harder to concentrate and to follow his instructions. The room felt like a freezer and I was scared I'd pass out in the room. *What will he do? Call an ambulance? How will Chris know if I am OK?*

'Cover yourself with this blanket,' he said holding a large folded blanket in front of me.

But I knew the signs. No amount of breathing would still my trembling limbs. The past 12 months had been a nightmare. At times like these, in the depths of my despair, anxiety was my solace; it kept me on high alert. That vicious cycle would crush me and I would fight back. Anxiety and I had a fierce love–hate relationship.

But we were close to the end of this session and this called for desperate measures to fix my rattled state.

'Come with me,' Geoff said, jumping up from his seat. 'You need some healing.'

In the big room he quickly set up the table and soon I was on the bed while he lit the incense and started the singing bowls.

'Do whatever you must to settle yourself,' he said with such urgency that I felt myself moving around to get comfortable. This was the time for me to be brutal in confronting my anxiety.

While he created the calmness in the room, I searched for the gaps between the thoughts racing around. Conversations from my past swirled, filling the crevices of my mind. There was only one way to slow my thoughts down — access that space of stillness.

I had to surrender to the sacredness in the room created by the sound of the singing bowls, and prayer., I repeated the mantra Ma-ra-na-tha until my muscles relaxed. My teeth had stopped clattering, my jaw unclenched and my breathing slowed. Drifting on the cloud, my body softened and a warm glow filled every cell. Peace soon filled my mind and soul.

This time we were able to move through the events of my life with an urgency. The thoughts were still there but by following my breath and witnessing it, I drifted from the past to this sacred, precious present moment. Bliss, at last.

WHEN I OPENED MY EYES, at the end of the session, the room looked brighter and my eye pain had settled. Geoff looked pleased with the work we were able to get through and his gentle smile was back in place. We sat in silence for a little while until he spoke about my next appointment and strategies to use over the next week. His determination to get me through my traumatic memories, had facilitated the release of the continuing heaviness clouding my mind. Another turning point in his work with me.

So many times, I had feared that he would give up and put me in the too hard basket. But he surprised me by continually offering strategies, using energy work, and spirituality to get me through each session. This was no mean feat for someone working with a complex, over-thinker like me. Or as Geoff so eloquently put it, someone who is sensitive to emotion. In other words, high on neuroticism.

Once home, nausea filled my body. Exhausted and emotionally drained, I slept for several hours and woke up around midnight. In the stillness of the night, writing was my companion. The words flowed. Almost manically, I spent several hours writing, releasing emotions that had been stuck. My body felt deeply calm, a radiance had crept down from my face through my arms and legs and down into my fingers and toes.

Over the next week, as I moved through each day, my mind eagerly tuned into my body to feel the changes. I noticed a little more stillness and calmness, less reaction, more gratitude, kindness, patience, more ease and grace as I started each day.

I could now lose myself in 45-minute meditation sessions. Negative thoughts and energy around the traumatic memories had lessened and were less distracting. I had accessed my pain, as Geoff often reminded me, and brutally confronted the negative thoughts. Now I could see and moderate the fluctuations. The ability to access this calm place was pure and precious.

THE EYE TRAUMA HAD TO BE TREATED. When the doctor had to perform emergency laser surgery on my eye the next day, I was in a much better headspace to cope with this unexpected turn of events. Weeks later when the specialist finally gave me the all clear, I almost knocked him off his feet when I leaped out of my chair to hug him. He was clearly not used to such exuberance!

CHAPTER FOURTEEN
GRIEF, UNSPOKEN

Everyone can master a grief but he that has it.

— WILLIAM SHAKESPEARE

NOTHING IS SIMPLE AFTER DEATH.

I have always loved playing cards. Frances and I were the biggest cheaters and always wound up as partners in a game. We had developed skills in a card game called *Klawerjas*; something we learned in South Africa. We worked out secret signs.

On the weekend before she died, we played cards. Frances and I and our husbands made up the foursome. She was the counter and I was the support player. She touched the mole on her hand and I knew she had the trump card, the Jack in the deck. We were set to win. Our husbands struggled to fathom how we won so many games.

The Jack of any suit now reminds me of death. Shuffling cards now reminds me, too. Ordinary things that we found funny have now completely altered for me. I no longer play cards. Grief has rearranged how I feel about a deck of cards. Maybe in time, I will play Uno or Donkey and learn new skills with a new partner.

Grief was part of my life from the age of six. When my younger brother, Owen, died I was bewildered. I yearned to see him, to find out where he'd gone. Yet, no one spoke about death in our home. Mum struggled with her grief and her deep guilt about Owen drowning while he was in her care. Dad, devastated, coped with Owen's loss by remaining silent. There was always the silence; Owen's name was never mentioned after he died. Our family, particularly Mum, had to contend with her desolation alongside many well-meaning people reminding her that it was God's will and that Owen was an angel who belonged in heaven. She wiped her tears and appeared strong. It seemed a betrayal of our Catholic faith to show a broken heart. Mum had to cry in silence; there was always someone around who'd quieten her wailing.

Often, at night, in the dark, I'd stand by the table and touch his photograph. It was as if I could feel his presence and, when I moved, his eyes followed me. Grief was something that grew more intense as I aged and deepened further when I longed for our family to be together.

THE CHURCH ASKED THE GRIEF STRICKEN to not weep or question the will of God. I never understood that. I had a right to be angry and sad, to cry and to question my devastation. Thoughts and prayers were not going to help me to find answers or give me comfort. I needed to work through it my way, on my terms.

When my Dad died several years later, I wept for weeks. I was not ready to let go when he closed his eyes for the last time. Death separated us forever. And that made me angry.

'Your father is in a better place,' said the priest. 'He is resting where no shadows fall.'

'How do you know that,' I asked through my tears. 'The church tells us about purgatory — the place where all souls languish. I don't want my Dad's soul to be in that place.'

The priest and I had many conversations but they invariably ended with him steering me to scripture. I was supposed to dry my tears and think that my father was just in another room. But if he was, that room was not in our house.

DEATH IS A CERTAINTY and what I know is that the grieving process, which happens in our own time and own way, is what releases the pain and sadness. Some people have remarked that I may be stuck in my grief. I am not sure what the opposite of that is. 'You have to move on for your own sake' was a common remark. The poignancy lay in the fact that the person I wanted to talk to about it all, was no longer there.

Perhaps being stuck in grief means I talk about my siblings and my father like they are still with me. I reminisce about our lives together and what bound our family. I still cry when I hear a song or when I realise they're no longer here in the flesh. Thinking of them is such a natural thing for me that when I think of them, it's just a part of my present and continuing life. I am not stuck when I openly miss them. Yet age has brought a better understanding of all of this as a part of life.

My Dad died before his actual death. His years of breathing difficulties had ravaged his body and he'd given up the will to live. It was hell to watch my spirited father struggle and see him weaken before my eyes. His asthma medication no longer provided relief. I'd hear him at night labouring to breathe. I felt as if I was dying alongside him. But all I wanted to do was talk to him — about anything.

In the days before my Dad's funeral, while Frances and George made the funeral arrangements, I rearranged all my books. My father loved words and I had a deep need, in the first few days after he died, to unpack, repack and arrange my books in alphabetical order.

To lessen my pain, I had to talk about my Dad. I wanted to laugh at the things he'd said, be angry on his behalf at the dark injustices of apartheid. I wanted to share his love of sport, his outspokenness. I wanted to retell the hilarious story of him sleeping on the floor in their bedroom where the bed was when he left for work but wasn't, when he came back. Mum often rearranged the furniture in the house to change the environment.

I mentally recorded many of our conversations and stored many other things in the crevices of my mind so I could tell our next generation. His quirkiness and his brilliance were characteristics that I treasured.

In the 1980s, we moved to Australia. When George died suddenly in 1993, at 39, leaving a 10-year-old daughter without a father, the searing grief engulfed me. George had lived a fast and furious life, and fitted in things that might take most people a lifetime. But he was young when his alcoholism took its toll. His body had collapsed under his addiction.

My despair churned in the pit of my stomach, filled me with rage. I wanted to lash out at him for abusing his body. Watching his 10-year-old daughter wail at his coffin, pierced my heart. *How can life be so cruel? Where is God? Owen was only 4! Dad was only, 60!*

It was very hard that here in our new country, no one knew George. I couldn't talk to them about him, laugh at his antics, express my anger and frustration at his early death, or share stories of our escapades. We had left behind the family and friends with whom we could share our grief. And George was now someone not many of our Australian community knew; a person only we could talk about, long for and want to see. Now, we had only photographs as reminders of a shared life.

Nothing could have prepared me for further devastation in our family. While still in deep mourning for George, and without warning my sister, Frances, was diagnosed with terminal cancer. It felt like a nightmare. She seemed fine one day; and within a week, after saying she had pain in her back and arm, she was admitted to hospital with advanced cancer. They located a tumour in her spine, but it was the secondary cancer, and it led to discovering the primary as breast cancer.

FRANCES'S BATTLE WAS LONG and debilitating but she defied her medical prognosis and battled for 15 years. She had several periods of remission but only a miracle could save her. I, however, remained optimistic when Mum and my siblings faltered. I was led by a blind faith that she would survive; I kept everyone's spirits up.

As sisters, Frances and I shared a special bond and a unique language: words and sentences that evoked fits of laughter until we gasped for breath. Morning two-hour phone calls, preceded by visits the previous evening were a regular. Our dinner tables were always laid with extra places in case someone arrived unannounced.

'Remember when you saw me in the train,' she said and was almost crying with laughter, 'and I was wearing your favourite dress without your permission?'

'You probably got away with it so many times before that fateful day when I left work early and got on the same train.'

'Remember when you got into trouble for cutting your hair,' she'd remind me.

'And then I blamed you.'

We had hours of listening, sharing, debating, arguing, gossiping, and laughing. Age did not diminish our vocabulary, it merely catapulted it into new spheres of wisdom and wonderment. A shared journey of marriages, childbirths, raising families, juggling careers, and business ventures. When the shadow of death lurked, it changed our language into medical terms and words of fear. But the laughter never stopped — it was silenced only by her last breath.

MY CONFIDANTE, MY BEST FRIEND and, with me, the one holding the family together, was not allowed to leave. We were supposed to retire together and had promised to move in together should we outlive our husbands. My faith in God took a further beating. *How are we serving a loving God when our family is suffering so much?* She cannot die. I am not ready to lose another sibling.

Despite the fears, I pushed on with living a life as normal as possible. We celebrated Christmas, birthdays and family concerts together. Frances never lost her feisty spirit and her outspoken opinions. She remained positive that she would beat cancer. One day in hospital after she'd had had several chemotherapy treatments she said to Mum, 'Brush my hair and tie it up.'

In one swift movement, Mum, standing behind her, gently lifted Frances's hair as piles of it fell into Mum's hands. Our eyes locked, and Mum's terror matched mine. Stomach churning, familiar vibrations in my body, and the room suddenly looking darker. *Breathe. Don't panic, just breathe.*

'I wonder when I'll start losing my hair?' Frances looked at us. 'Do you think it'll grow back straight?' She giggled.

Any words stuck in my throat. My eyes shifted back to Mum, with her hands full of hair.

'Just put it in a ponytail,' Frances said as she lifted her hand to smooth her hair.

Her eyes darted from me to her hand then she turned around to face Mum who stood with tear-filled eyes and wads of hair. The hospital staff came running as Frances's wailing filled the ward.

In that moment, I found strength as I hugged Mum and removed the hair from her hands. It was a pivotal moment for the three of us, in accepting the enormity of Frances's battle.

I remained optimistic that she'd bounce back and she did, many times, and her hair grew back and fell out again. But her strength and resilience were remarkable.

Frances started sewing and painting, despite pain and fatigue. She made doona covers and tablecloths and painted fabric. After recovering from her first chemotherapy program I watched her shakily balance on her favourite high-heeled shoes. Her legs were so thin that I worried about her falling and breaking a limb.

As Frances swung between death's door and living, we grew closer. My own fears were pushed aside and I tried to be there for her as much as I could. We still had laughs and long phone calls. She was the keeper of my secrets, the outspoken, swear-like-a-trooper sister.

When a friend remarked that someone's 'time was up' I was enraged. 'By whose decree?', I asked.

Towards the end, my anxiety levels heightened. I was not ready to let go of her and was determined to stay positive. My nightmares were at their worst, and visits to Dr Abdurahman increased.

He was very sympathetic; worked with me through my darkness as I struggled with Frances's diagnosis. Not once did he question my insecurities or my paranoia. His dry sense of humour and patient manner carried me through many fearsome moments. He was diligent and examined me to check for back or breast pain and was at pains to reassure me. His room was a place where my tears flowed freely and also, where my mood often could shift from dark to light. Sometimes, to lighten the situation, he'd reach into his draw and jokingly pull out a treat he kept for children.

Frances's condition deteriorated, however, I remained hopeful she could fight the disease. Mum tried to prepare herself for the loss of her third child, and during our conversations the pain was etched in her voice.

In Frances's last days in palliative care, I walked into her room and saw a book on her bed. *What happens to us when we die?* I was being forced to confront my fear of death and of her death. I felt sick and dizzy.

Around me, heart monitors beeped, nurses moved around, and patients murmured. Somehow, I remained frozen at her bedside. I wanted to grab the book and toss it out the window.

'Did you come by train?' she said as she opened her eyes. I knew she was in a confused state.

'Let's get the ball and play some soccer on the field,' she continued.

This was something we did at the back of our childhood

home. Smiling, I said she was in hospital and we didn't have a ball.

'I am going to die,' she said when she caught me staring at the book.

'Don't say that. You don't know that.'

FRANCES DIED AFTER THE EASTER WEEKEND. I had spent the weekend with her as had her husband, always at her bedside. On the Sunday, it settled in my mind that she would not recover. On that fateful day, we had laughed so much that we left the ward so as not to disturb the other patients. We told each other funny stories and laughed until she wet herself and I gasped for air. Frances was hooked to an oxygen tank; her ravaged body could no longer cope with any further treatment.

On Tuesday 6 April, death stole another member of our family. *I don't know where to go from here. I am holding on by a thread.*

AS I KNEW I HAD TO, I went about my life, working, taking care of my family, talking to Mum every day, sometimes three or four times. But at odd times, in odd places, I was hit by the grief. In the supermarket, at the hairdressers. I wanted to wear a sign: My sister just died. In the bathroom at work or the privacy of my bedroom, I bawled my eyes out. She was not only my sister but also my best friend. She was a spirited, complex person that not many people understood. She was the one constant in my life. Frances's death hit me the hardest of all my losses.

In this our new country, we did not have the luxury of extended family support. She was ever conscious, not of her own demise, but that **her** death would expose our children to a family funeral.

When Frances died, our family fell apart. She would have been devastated that her death caused so much unnecessary heartache. For years, we could not talk about her death without the family rift rearing its head. The reality surrounding her death held a heaviness that none of us knew how to change. We battled through loss, each in our own way, each in agony and despair. We were all desperately in need of grief counselling.

I chose silence. It pained me to talk about her death to anyone.

The death of those we love changes us. It changed me. At times I avoided people so that I did not have to talk about Frances's death. People started avoiding me... my pain was so intense. Friendships can end. Friends often cannot cope with you talking about your loved one which, for us, is a release. Even when people want to support, they are often ill-equipped to do so.

When I talk about my family, all my siblings are included as if they are still here. The non-grieving world doesn't always understand this.

The reality of grief is far different from what most people see from the outside. At times, it felt as if time had stopped. At times nothing feels real. Some are judged because they are not mourning long enough. Some for mourning for too long. There are hard days, a song or a treasured photograph instantly brings tears. Then there are days where I can laugh at reminders of my Dad and siblings. Death and grieving have no bounds.

I am, now, even more protective of those remaining than I ever was. I shifted from my middle child status to that of the oldest. So, I love and protect my family with a fierceness that death cannot diminish.

WHEN I FINALLY HAD THE COURAGE to talk to Geoff about my grief, a great relief swept over me. My grief belongs to me yet, in a small psychology room in the Sutherland Shire, sitting on a couch opposite someone who looked at me with such kindness, I could unleash the pain and confusion, my anger and frustration at God. The space, offered a safe haven where my tears could flow and wet tissues would fill his waste paper basket.

At first, I tried hard to hide my vulnerability. But as the weeks went by, through my tears, free of recrimination and judgement, this time offered me a sense of freedom to express my resentment at religion and how it forces us to bury our sorrow. Through my own struggle, I had discovered, how ill-equipped people are to deal with grieving people.

'No one could see this gaping hole that opened when Frances died,' I said.

Geoff nodded.

'When I cry in front of you, I am truly hurting,' I sobbed.

'That's OK,' Geoff said. 'There is nothing wrong with unleashing your pain in any way you feel comfortable.'

Through my red and swollen eyes, I could release the pain as if she'd died just a few moments ago. Everyone has lost someone. Wounded, pain ravaged people are everywhere among us. That pain can still be as real many years later, as if it had just happened. I am not mourning the tragic death of someone but rather it's the wound that remains ever present. I mourn openly, and sometimes hang by a thread. It's hard to articulate our fear about our loss and grief.

The answer is not to hide pain and just 'suck it up'. Rather, grieving is meant to happen; loudly if we wish, and for as long as we need.

In the park next door to my house, I often encounter a woman who visits her family down our street. She is still grieving her adult son who died 16 years ago and she tears up when she repeats the story of his death. As we watch her grandchildren play, we share our feelings about our pain.

AFTER THE HYPNOTHERAPY SESSIONS, it had become easier to speak of my despair and face my fears of death and of losing any more of my family. The words continued to tumble out of my mouth. It was a relief to articulate my fear of dying, and my recurrent nightmares about drowning that plagued me since childhood. And sometimes, it felt weird, somewhat crazed to discuss these fears as rational feelings.

'Can you please help me to cope when these feelings overwhelm me?' I asked. I don't know how to handle my grief when it surfaces.'

'I suggest you prepare some rituals to remember them by,' he said. 'Think of their favourite things or special dates that you would like to turn into times where you can reminisce.'

'I always talk to my Mum on their birthdays or the anniversary of death,' I said. 'It's so comforting to remember the things about them that only we can laugh at and understand.'

What supported me most was that Geoff listened. I could unpack my deepest fears, work through my resentment towards God without Geoff trying to convince me that what had happened was 'meant to be'. I so desperately needed the space to feel free of shame and guilt and to be as vulnerable as I needed.

I was coming to terms with there being no shame in having an inner battle and continually projecting an image of a vulnerable person. Strength does not mean bearing our burden in silence; vulnerability and shame are as real as life is. We have choices about getting up after being knocked down and starting to walk again.

During one of my therapy sessions, I felt so pained about what had happened to our family, I lashed out at them. I wanted my Dad and siblings to know how angry I was about them dying. Though irrational, I turned my anger on myself for being angry. In the confines of the therapy room, that irrational behaviour felt justified. I was allowed to scream about my sadness and to express my distress about death.

Throughout, Geoff listened before gently steering me into what was rational thinking. Many times, it was not what he said but his caring gestures, the tone of his voice and the empathy in his eyes that made the difference for me.

While Geoff often talked about our individual soul's journey, he had the sensitivity to allow me to speak my truth, cry and mourn and take steps towards recovery.

Working with him led me to confront some painful memories that had impeded my ability to accept the loss of my family. While he reminded me that grief never goes away, he encouraged me to develop strategies to cope in those vulnerable moments of my fear, rage, sadness all of it. The most helpful strategy for me, was talking. And in his practice, in that sacred space, I could release my anguish, speak about my pain and confront my fears.

CHAPTER FIFTEEN
OUTSIDE OF MY POWER

*Out of suffering have emerged the strongest souls;
the most massive characters are seared with scars.*

— KAHLIL GIBRAN

A SENSE OF PEACE SURROUNDED ME in the weeks after my trauma therapy with Geoff had ended. My panic attacks were now rare and my anxiety levels manageable. Most nights, the nightmares subsided even though, most nights, sleep evaded me. I was no longer so intensely focused on my dreams and goals. For some reason, there was a space, perhaps even a hollowness, and an uncanny self-possession.

'Everything has shifted. Have I outgrown the person I once was?' I asked Geoff. 'Is this possible? Now that I've confronted these things, will my life come together again?'

Geoff answered that while my energy levels and enthusiasm had returned, I now needed to fill the gaps left by stopping my many projects. I was still isolated socially, and fearful. Despite being almost completely independent, driving, going about my daily life, some things were still challenging. Sitting in a crowded restaurant or sometimes even at the dinner table still made me uneasy.

These past few months, my lack of control and social ineptness was confusing. The despair about quitting my community events, the community choir and charity projects intensified.

Also, though I'd previously failed after many previous applications, I had finally been awarded a community grant to start a youth music ensemble. So I was deeply disappointed when I wasn't well enough to accept the grant.

'How do I make place for all these things, grief, relief, joy, work, family and friends?' I wanted to know. 'I haven't seen my family and friends for many months. Maybe the invitations will stop. It's like I've landed in a new country and have to learn a new culture, a new language and find my way around,' I said.

GEOFF, SENSING THAT MY MOOD was on a downward spiral, steered the conversation towards preparations for my two upcoming events. My last speaking engagement had been six months earlier. Now, with my confidence at rock bottom, the thought of talking about my book and answering questions no longer interested me.

It was time to capitalise on my renewed strength and my tentative, but belief in my abilities. Time to face the public again. Much of one therapy session was spent on putting strategies in place on how to deal with any unexpected questions from the audience and what my focus would be. The session ended with a deeply spiritual healing session leaving me ready for the presentation the next day.

On arrival at the school for my talk, the premises had been placed into lockdown. Usually this would have sent me into a panic attack. But since my recovery therapy, this was now easier to manage. While I knew I wasn't out of the woods yet, the triggers no longer controlled me.

'Mother, you attract these things, I'm not going anywhere with you again, I don't have words for you,' Sasha roared with laughter. 'These things can only happen to you. Say no more, I don't want to know.'

'It's really not funny.'

'But Mum, you are like a trauma magnet.'

'I'm cursed,' I said. 'I don't have to tell you that.' 'You are not cursed,' she laughed. 'There is no evil witch circling around you dishing out curses.'

'How do you explain the lift incident?'

'I know, that was uncanny,' she said.

'You were there with me in the lift.'

'But I had to get out to get Charlotte's formula.'

'And boom, just like that the glass lift is suspended in the air for all shoppers to see?'

'You and a screaming baby,' she laughs.

'That's the curse – and now, you're free from it.'

'I remember the emergency workers prising the door open just enough to get Charlotte out.'

'Yes, then leaving me behind in a panicked state,' I said.

She roared with laughter again.

AS I HEADED INTO THE AUDITORIUM, I felt nervous about facing an audience. Sasha, as always, a pillar of strength, positioned herself in my sightline to urge me on.

After my introduction, when I informed the audience that this was my first talk after several months in isolation, it set the mood, leaving me more relaxed to breathe life into my presentation. I looked over the crowd, and a sense of comfort arose. I'd intended to keep the talk low-key, but once in the zone, I unleashed my thoughts about the horrors of the past; the dehumanising aspect of apartheid and the responsibility white South Africans had towards restitution. While I knew an acknowledgement of responsibility, even an apology would have been a good gesture, it didn't change anything. There was so much more that the white privileged population could do to alleviate the pain of the disadvantaged.

WHEN PEOPLE ASK ME what they can do to help heal the past, my answer is simple. Admit to your privilege and the fact that you were protected while at the same time, participating in some level of oppression. Often, those who are privileged do not understand. Oppression destroyed lives, destroyed dreams, it separated families and is responsible for millions of our people, still today, living in abject poverty. My main message was that the privileged might need to be thankful that the oppressed can forgive.

'How do you feel towards white people now?' an audience member asked. 'I'm asking this because my grandparents were victims of the holocaust and they felt much resentment towards the perpetrators.'

'It's something I am working on. I don't hate them; but I do have a strong sense of resentment towards their privilege.'

I thought back to that moment in therapy when Geoff challenged me, and realised that we all have triggers that take us back to a time and place, no matter how deeply we bury these things.

When I read a confronting chapter from my book detailing my outrage when as a young woman in South Africa, I realised that we were trapped in a toxic situation, and there seemed no hope of a change. The audience listened intently and encouraged me to continue reading. That particular chapter detailed the humiliation of segregated life and the dehumanising aspect that most white South Africans either ignored or claimed to be oblivious to. I felt that familiar rage coursing through my limbs.

These same feelings of outrage had surfaced over the months after my book launch. The discussions and reviews on topics in my book, had set this harsher tone towards white privilege. My message about the injustices grew stronger. In particular, those regarding my parents and our generation, severely disadvantaged while other citizens lived richer lives based on their skin colour.

For me, humility and acceptance of what was, had been replaced with how much suffering those years caused and were still causing. I realised that this would open me up to more abuse from those who didn't agree with reopening old wounds. Many of our previous oppressors, while living outside of South Africa, were focused on the current democratic society. Enraged, they called me shallow and naïve. Chastising me for turning a blind eye to what was happening in South Africa now and questioning my view from the safety of my Australian home.

'DO YOU REGRET WRITING THE BOOK?' Geoff asked during a session.

'You've asked this question a few times,' I said. 'The short answer is no. The long answer is more complex.'

'Do you feel there's more focus on the past than on your family story?' he asked.

'I have had many excellent reviews but also many unkind comments about my family,' I said. 'People wondering where the adults, particularly my Mum, were when my brother Owen drowned. I would hate for my Mum to see that.'

'I've also had disgusting comments about my lineage that I can't repeat,' I said.

'When I read your book, you mentioned how you were brainwashed into aspiring to be like white South Africans to succeed in life,' he said. 'I find that incredible. What did you gain by doing that?'

'I don't expect you to understand what is was like,' I said. 'It was an upbringing thing. But if you must know back there was no way to process the feelings; then, only white people could afford therapy!'

My reason for writing this book was purely to record our family history. It was also to fulfil my childhood dream to write and publish a book. It was important to have this resource to let our future generations know why we are here, our family tree, the sacrifices we made to leave the country of our birth and set up home here, and the reasons for that. The thought that our history would be forgotten urged me on. Our stories, our history must be kept alive for generations to come.

'You know, I've read a lot of posts on social media with loads of advice on how to overcome my anxiety,' I said. 'At times it makes me feel like a freak, unable to take control. Those posts seem to make it so simple to move on and be normal, whatever that is.'

'That's the danger with social media,' he said. 'Too many experts. Try not to let that distract you from your own healing path.'

'Yes, it's distracting to read something telling me to 'fake it until I make it,' I said. 'Another platitude is, Don't sweat the small stuff. It's such an odd expression because it diminishes my pain.'

Many motivational books left me feeling more depressed and broken than relived or inspired. Even though I was traumatised, I was still highly motivated and pushed myself to succeed. My trauma made me more hypervigilant, it was a survival technique. At times, intensely self critical because I had such high standards, such an impossibly high need to please. This so often backfired on me. Despite my best efforts and my success, I never felt that I achieved anything. And then, my father's words often rang in my ears. 'Don't let the oppressors control your mind.'

'Trauma causes the nervous system to fight, freeze or flee,' said Geoff.

'That is why, these well meaning books and stuff, telling me to stay positive are cruel when I'm fighting for my sanity,' I said.

'Positive thinking is good but it can hide the reality that people sometimes feel out of control,' he said.

'So, it *is* OK not to feel OK, right?'

'Of course, It's OK not to feel OK, but we must learn to deal with what is not making us OK,' he said.

'Another frustrating thing is when people tell me to just let it go,' I said. 'It is a big deal when online trolls make nasty comments. I can't just let it go.'

'Yes. You're holding onto trauma and we are helping to drag it into the light, process it, talk about it and work on ways to get past it,' he said.

'And it's bloody painful,' I cried.

'Yes, it will be painful and uncomfortable and you'll have a period of grieving, but talking through it will help,' he said. 'Letting go will happen in its own time.'

I had become an expert at burying whatever I felt. But the pain never went away. Perhaps I would never heal because dissociation was easier than having to face what was so terrifying. Not sweating the small stuff was suggesting, to me, to shut down my emotions. It meant silence but also a greater build up of the trauma. Sometimes it's what others might call 'the small stuff' that's the crux of my trauma. Something as seemingly tiny as not being able to walk into a shop on my own.

THIS HEALING JOURNEY has allowed me to strip the layers from the surface and go deeper. Go into the months of intense isolation and deep-rooted fear. I had felt chosen by some enemy force, ramming me into a deep, dark hole. I had been floundering for so long that sometimes I felt like an ant crushed under the weight of my uncontrollable fears. But I had to go deep enough to look at what was festering and have the courage to confront it and heal it.

My analytical brain needed to repeat, process, and deconstruct some of the strategies before I could make sense of my patterns. Geoff's diagrams, spiritual guidance and energy healing sessions, in-depth explanations, patience and utmost empathy for my racing mind, allowed me to lift my wings up. Only now I had to trust myself to fly again.

I was growing, inside, like never before. Though for many years I'd been functioning at incredibly high levels, driven by an obsession to soar, I was ill-equipped for any setbacks. So when my resolve crumbled, I tormented myself and it led to self-destruction. All the chaos in my mind refused to let any good in, stopped me thinking about or relishing my achievements. Instead, I questioned why I was even in this world. Then, why I'd allowed the events of the past year to rock the axis of my being.

Shame and vulnerability had played a big part in my suffering and hampered my ability to open up during therapy. To overcome them, I needed to be brave about owning my weaknesses. This was something I struggled with in therapy. To share about this area of my life needed forgiveness and acceptance of self. As a coping mechanism it had become easier for me to bury my shame.

Now, slowly, I felt profoundly reassured. I understood, in a profound way, that challenges happen to people — good people and bad people. And with this renewed calm, positive thoughts crept in as did an alignment with a sense of purpose. These moments arose when I stopped fighting life and stopped forcing my journey into what I thought it should be. What surprised me the most, perhaps is that gratitude and grace came naturally. What I had perceived as impossible, became possible.

Incredibly, the joy of writing had returned and with it, my daily practice. I had found immense joy and purpose in writing a new book. My focus was now solely on writing about my journey of self-discovery and healing in the hope that someone else who may be struggling would seek help much sooner than I did.

Through working with Geoff's belief and approach to healing the mind and the spirit, I had been given new strategies to cope with my fears. My diet had improved and the healing instilled so much calmness and radiance in my mind. For the first time in many years, there was a light that could guide me out of the darkness.

There were interesting times, too, in working with Geoff when I felt my ego was being challenged. Letting go of the person I had perceived as me, was the hardest. Many times, I struggled with Geoff's clinical opinion over what I believed was his empathy of my world. And, he continually showed such profound insight (and empathy) into how we were connecting and building trust within these challenging scenarios.

The challenges we face, be they discrimination on the basis of gender, race, ethnicity, or religious beliefs cause much distress. The message from many would be to ignore these challenges, build up a resistance by turning a blind eye or simply walking away from them. To my thinking, those suffering trauma need to do more than that. When the world appears a cruel place, many people who function at high levels, turn to substance abuse, or suffer depression, anxiety, disease, withdrawal as a way to cope with the pain of what they see, or have been indoctrinated to believe, is a failure on their part. For some, tragically, an escape from this world is the only solution to their pain.

For me, the support and growing strength from venturing deep within myself and the courage to confront my demons was the way to douse the raging fire inside. I confronted my anxiety and panic disorder head on; realised that a healthier happier life was possible. To raise my wings up I had to embrace a belief in a sacredness of life so I could go to new heights.

Since launching *A Darker Shade of Pale*, and having to face my fears head on, my smile had disappeared. I was exhausted by the weight of years of burying my fears. By removing my mask, I had opened a place for fear, loneliness, shame, exhaustion; and rage. And my body told me it could no longer hold these pressures. That I would need to begin again.

Many times, I wanted to switch to 'mere survival' mode — far more appealing than this bewildering state.

'Is it possible for someone to just bury the trauma and live their best life?' I asked Geoff. 'Have you seen that happen in your work?'

'Yes, there's certainly an aspect of that,' he offered. 'We can't be happy all the time. We'll be depressed from time to time. Problems flare up. One person will be struggling with anxiety, another might recognise they've got an addictive tendency. So yes, at times we need to accept our problems, not really the same as bury them, but it does mean we just get on with life.'

He looked at the picture on the wall for a few seconds and then trained his eyes on me. 'And sometimes going into 'survival mode' … just getting back to work even though you are still a little depressed will help you function and overcome the depression. Often the worst thing a person with depression can do is take time off work as it gives them way too much thinking time. So, it's a balance between processing things and at the same time "faking it until you make it". Too much processing and the person can be avoiding, plastering over a large problem by talking about a smaller one.'

This was a lot to process, but it made sense. For the moment, I had a more pressing question.

'How can I stay motivated when the darkness looms?' I asked.

'Practice gratitude. Always consider how far you've come. It's as simple as counting your blessings and not focusing on what you are missing,' he said.

'I find it hard,' I said. 'Good things don't cancel out the horrible things. They occupy the same space in my life.'

When he mentioned gratitude, I felt guilty at my lack of it. The past year I'd allowed myself to be robbed of my gratitude for realising my lifelong dream of writing a book. So many good things were happening around me, good reviews and media interviews, encouraging messages from readers… but my mind focused on the negativity. When the horrible incidents surfaced, the painful memories of life under oppression and the online attacks demeaning my ancestry, it was extremely hard to remain grateful.

Practising gratitude for my achievements wasn't part of my busy life. My quiet moments only led to a hunger to accomplish more. It was a frantic energy; it squashed the sense of appreciation for everything around me. The energy went into pushing and encouraging my family to reach for the stars, into listening to the problems of the world. And I had none left to witness the abundance in my own life. In times of despair my heart, which was often open for others, was closed to myself.

'I'D LIKE TO GO BACK to living my best life,' I said. 'When I struggle to do the simple things — jumping in my car to meet a friend for coffee, sit down in a café without squirming in my seat, just laugh and talk for hours — then I think it will never happen.'

'So, the things we've done in therapy — facing your past and looking at it without regret — will prepare you for the future without fear,' he said. 'It may sound simple, but it's about trusting the process and living in the moment with confidence.'

Facing that past had allowed me to see how much it had contributed to my pain. At the root of it was an upbringing survival rule: *Be the best you can be despite the odds stacked against you.*

When I felt a hint of failure, I grew it into unhappiness. I ensured there was no time to breathe. So I ran like hell and poured my heart and soul into showbusiness while my untreated anxiety and panic disorder worsened. My internal compass could no longer cope with the changes of direction I was forcing it to make.

While the decision to retire from my job at the university had been driven by a challenging situation in the workplace — my workplace was no longer a healthy environment — it had undermined my confidence. And the bash to my ego was the hardest part to deal with.

But being boosted by writing *A Darker Shade of Pale* I saw that having available space also meant full-time writing was possible.

GETTING BACK TO UNDERSTANDING how I'd reached that place meant seeing how I truly operated in the world. What seemed to fill my heart, was creating happiness and opportunities for others. When I failed to help a choir from Cape Town attend an event I was working on for the NSW State Government, I decided to set up my own events company. This was purely to create opportunities for previously disadvantaged artists to come to Australia.

My drive to be of service came from growing up with the deprivation that I had. So, I wanted to make a difference in the lives of those less fortunate in the world. I believed that true happiness, joy and freedom evolved from serving others. Only the serving knew no bounds. I didn't stop where most people would.

Somehow, even the intensity of this effort gave me comfort that I hadn't abandoned my roots. It kept me connected to that tree my parents had planted in the country of our birth. Many of my fundraising projects were to support those in Cape Town as a reminder of my connection; of my love for it. This love was like a burning light that nothing could extinguish. It was time to come out of the darkness and shine my light once again.

On visits back to Cape Town, I witnessed the same levels of poverty that I'd experienced growing up. It strengthened my resolve to help others. Sometimes, this was even to my own disadvantage. I had no ulterior motive, sought no reward, other than making people happy.

I looked for worthwhile projects to make this service a reality. A few years ago, I came across someone knitting trauma teddy-bears on my train. An idea popped into my head and set off a new project to tackle. I'd seen a newsletter from an organisation supporting HIV/AIDS infected and affected children in South Africa asking for support. Knitting groups sprang up all around the country. Within weeks my loungeroom was filled with more than 3000 teddy-bears. The colourful teddy-bears ended up on display in NSW Parliament House during the screening of a movie about HIV/AIDS.

When I started the project, I had given no thought to how I'd get one teddy-bear to the orphanage, let alone 3000. The teddy-bears eventually found their way into many organisations in South Africa.

Every visit to South Africa presented another opportunity for charitable projects. One such was to take a group from an isolated and deprived township to a concert. Again, I had no idea how I would pull it off. But, through a fundraising drive in the expat community, I raised enough money to take a group of seniors to a concert in Cape Town's biggest casino. There was enough money to hire a bus, buy tickets to the show and treat the group to a sumptuous dinner.

Ventures like these were the meaningful things missing from my life. It weighed heavily that if I cared for myself, I may not be able to give so much to others. But I had to make the decision, this time, to start with my own wellbeing. I cried many tears in Geoff's room about being unable to keep going with these projects. At least, for that time.

THE MORE I LEARNED to appreciate my true worth without continually judging myself or focusing on the areas where I'd failed to achieve, the more available a healthy psyche seemed to be. With Geoff's guidance, I had been given the keys to unlock the many cells in my prison and it was now up to me to open it. The keys had to fit for me to open those prison doors.

The challenge? My mindset had to shift from surviving to thriving. My ingrained habits were lodged deeply in my mind and dislodging them would need a fearless determination. As I discovered during therapy, that dislodging is liberating.

The missing piece of the puzzle was my lack of self-love. The need to project love and care towards others was, in turn, depleting my caring for myself. My ego — paramount to my existence — needed nourishment though that was being dragged from my already worn-out soul. *How can I change this? What will others think if I am no longer available to them?*

Perhaps one incident, more than others, was the seat of the lack of self worth. I felt deep guilt about Owen's death. Vivid images still appeared and cracked me. Writing about the drowning brought to life the moments embedded in my unconscious mind. I relived the tragic details as a six-year-old.

During therapy, whenever we talked about Owen and how guilty I felt about that day, I had great difficulty staying still. I had to get up and move around the room. I couldn't face Geoff. I loathed myself in those moments; I felt deep shame that I'd failed Owen.

This was something I'd never discussed with anyone except Frances. She felt the same shame. She knew about my nightmares. None of my siblings can swim. Andy, who was born after Owen died, had never put his feet in the water. Maureen who was three months old when Owen died also tried at various times but was always afraid.

After Sasha was born, I was determined to learn how to swim while she was learning. Mum went along with me to lessons. But when the moment came to submerge my face in the water, it was excruciating. I couldn't. After a lesson at night my dreams would be filled with torturous swirling under water. I stopped going to swimming lessons.

WHEN GEOFF SUGGESTED A HEALING SESSION after an intense talk session, I was eager to find some peace. He spoke in such gentle tones whenever we talked about Owen. This healing session rattled my emotions initially. I felt uneasy about possibly seeing something or someone I didn't want to. With my eyes tightly closed, I listened to Geoff calling up our ancestors. This ritual was comforting and instilled the belief that I had their protection. I found myself drifting into my own realm, the place where the soft light glowed and warmed my cells. I relaxed as I anticipated the healing.

'Imagine that there is a bucket on the floor next to you,' I heard him say. 'Now allow the pain and guilt to drain from your body into the bucket.'

If I did, truly, want to release that guilt and pain I had to open my mind to this healing. I wanted this healing so much. I wanted to release Owen, to tell him how much I wished that he was still alive and how sorry I am that he drowned while we all played around him. Geoff's comforting tone allowed me to visualise a place of beauty, of safety. I saw colourful flowers and birds flashing by. As the sound of the singing bowls filled the room, I felt a release. My limbs relaxed and a warmth spread through my arms and legs. An indescribable release of emotion drained from my cells. I willed the pain to drain from within me. As sobs racked my body, Geoff chanted. As the session ended, I opened my eyes and stared at the ceiling until he moved from his seat on the floor.

Back in his room, we sat until I had composed myself. Then, we discussed how I felt during the healing. I felt it had brought a release, a deep comfort and an acceptance. I had finally uncovered layers of guilt and confusion embedded in my young mind since the drowning.

The calm was immediate, after the session, but it was only weeks later that I felt the true effects. I had forgiven myself and felt a deep sense of peace. I longed for this kind of peace to flow through all my memories.

DURING CHALLENGING PERIODS IN THERAPY, it was easier to regress into narratives like, 'I don't want to go there because it's too painful,' or, 'I've tried so many things to change my thinking but nothing works'. But Geoff's encouragement increased my perseverance and the resolve, 'It's now or never,' kept me strong and determined to conquer the fear.

Being stuck in dread drained my ability to love myself and to create real happiness; a state where I would be the beneficiary. It was a challenge to acknowledge and live in a place where I could accept myself, be proud of my achievements, accept praise, love myself and find the radiance and beauty that lives in me. These qualities that I so easily bestowed on others to make them happy was vital to my own healing. This had to become my priority to truly fulfil my destiny.

My ego was battling; exposing the many reasons to remain in the clutches of anxiety. Whenever fear began to paralyse me, I had to focus on not succumbing to old habits. Staying on this journey of transformation would take a truckload of resilience and strength. And learning to do this without judgement or fear of failure would be crucial. The other vital element was the realisation that failure was not a bad thing; success came from getting up and trying again.

As Geoff often reminded me, setting goals, practising and continuing to practise would get me to the other side. I had to be courageous to release myself from the prison. I'd locked myself in, but underneath these layers, joy and happiness were waiting to come to the fore.

During a therapy session Geoff discussed methods of turning off negative thoughts. In that setting, the comfort of the therapy room, the ability to rewire my brain looked relatively straightforward. *How wrong I was.*

While Geoff is not the best artist, his diagrams were always interesting, and showed a clear strategy! One diagram included the many negative thoughts our mind processed daily. Thoughts of anger, fear, self-loathing, violence, judgement, etc. All these thoughts would have a big impact on what is going on around me and lead to my mind constantly being fed with this negativity.

'Do you sing?' he asked. 'Singing and music are some of the ways you can ward of negativity. When a negative thought pops up, it will prevent you from processing anything else around you,' he said. 'Try practising a positive thought to replace the negativity.'

'I think my negativity will need therapy if I sing,' I smiled.

During these lighter moments, Geoff often revealed more details of his own life and struggles. This made him seem so real, not a practitioner, but a fellow traveller. His genuine interest in helping me move through trauma to a sense of calm was a significant part of my continuing the healing process. That and, of course, a lot of work.

Learning to let go of negativity required work. Positive thoughts disappeared when anxiety shattered my confidence. Even when I had a small sense of control of anxiety, some panic would rear its head about losing that control. Especially in a public space.

And, in that past 12 months, I had lost a good deal of the meaning in my life. The overwhelming pressures and sudden decision to end all my activities had left a void. My life now no longer revolved around being important or doing extraordinary things.

CHAPTER SIXTEEN
FEELING AND HEALING

*Not everything that is faced can be changed
but nothing can be changed until it is faced.*

— JAMES BALDWIN

'REPEAT AFTER ME,' I said. 'I, Geoff Lyons, am thankful for my gift of healing. I promise to continue to use my gifts to help people.'

From his seat on the pillow, Geoff obligingly repeated my words.

'And so, it is,' I concluded.

'And so, it is.' And he smiled.

I had just shared my news with him that I'd be starting a post-graduate creative writing course. When I first arrived at therapy, I had abandoned my application and resigned myself to the idea that developing my writing skills further, would remain a dream. If someone had told me twelve months earlier, that this was possible, I would have cried.

Now following this life-changing healing, there was a renewed confidence, where my fears use to sit. My life felt radiant, now; I rejoiced. The sun shone through new and old clouds, warmed me and helped the tears, heartache and pain subside. I couldn't stop now. There could be no going back to that dark place where I tried to hide from the world.

For the first time in more than 50 years I was nightmare free. Chris, who'd only ever known me to have nightmares, often jokingly referred to them as my alien friends visiting during the night. When they did visit, I would hold onto him for fear of falling or drowning. Many nights he would shake me awake, sometimes needing to be quite vigorous, while I let out weird choking noises.

But now, though Chris still sometimes woke to check I was sleeping soundly, I slept through the night.

I had much to relish in my life. True beauty, love was all around me. But I'd been robbed of seeing it because of my continual search for fulfilment, for recognition, stemming from my earlier life of deprivation. My perceived failures, ever present, tricked me into a continuous flow of pleasing others. It boosted my ego, but being the 'go-to person' had also taken its toll.

The intense grief increased my loneliness and despair that, at the best of times, eroded my joy of living. My struggle to let go of my siblings who had died, crippled my thoughts. I still wished for a different outcome, even if I knew it was impossible. Death had a sting. It got into my eyes, crawled on my skin and remained shackled in my mind. We were not just family through our DNA. Our bond, like superglue, was unbreakable through all the highs and lows of life. Our childhood connection grew stronger with age. We followed each other to settle in a new country. Our motto was: Family over everything, and our inner circle, which others around us had named, was unbreakable. Only death could separate us. And when it did, I was left to grapple with the missing links, tried to apply solder and dance in the circle at whim constantly wanting to feel them around me.

I LEARNED THAT GRIEVING can be unpacked and talked through in therapy. For me that was only the beginning of the process. I needed to connect with my siblings, spiritually, to release them.

Through the healing sessions I could access the pain in a trusting environment; a space where I could release my anger and chastise God, Spirit and the universe. Somewhere someone would understand, without judgement, why this grief felt like it was killing me.

Being allowed to tell your truth in a trusting environment, being heard, validated and honoured is paramount for the grieving process. So often, acknowledgement of grief is all that is needed.

In therapy, Geoff exposed me to an alternate thought process. This was by no means easy to achieve. Though I'd hoped the process of unburdening would be instantly healing, it sent an uncontrollable fear through me that left my limbs rigid and fuelled a destructive chaos in my mind.

Fear, as always, was my biggest obstruction. Accessing my blockages meant getting my psyche to let go of its security blanket. At times, dredging up the fear, I was driven to leave a room, stand in a dark corner and wrap the blanket tighter around my pain. I think I was hoping to strangle it.

While talk therapy allowed me to access the pain, it was the healing energy in Geoff's hands that then surged through my cells, soothed my wounds and caressed my mind. This combination of healing led me on the path to recovery. Learning about mindfulness and accessing my thoughts in a meditative state allowed me to fully absorb the energy and embrace the healing.

And, despite the mountain ahead having many pathways, some narrow and winding that crushed my feet, others were wide open leading to a vastness that my senses longed to embrace. Reaching the top of the climb, hampered at times by the weight bearing, seemed unattainable. Each difficult moment left me with a torrent of hurt and anguish.

'Ask me that question now, whether I regret writing my book,' I lashed out.

'OK, do you regret writing that book?'

'Today, I hate it, I hate it.'

'Why?'

'Because it exposes so much about me, so much about how

wounded I am from the way I was forced to grow up. And now everything feels raw and painful, like it's still happening and I am trapped.'

'Do you know how it felt watching my colleagues eat in a café, when I couldn't go in. Do you know how it felt to be turned away from a hospital with a sick child because of our colour? Do you understand why I am so angry?'

'Yes' Geoff answered, 'I can understand your anger'. He stopped, looked away at the picture on the wall and turned back to me. 'What else are you angry about?'

'I'm angry at my siblings for leaving. I'm angry at my brother for succumbing to his lifestyle. I'm angry at God or the universe for robbing me of those that I love. It hurts.'

'It's natural to have those feelings.'

'I also get angry at myself for being angry. I don't know if you can understand that.'

'You are angry at yourself, huh.'

'I just want to remember them. Every day. I don't want to forget them and let them fade from my memory. We shared so much.'

I felt uncomfortable having to release these pent-up emotions to anyone. But Geoff's gentleness gave me the confidence. I spoke about some of the things that felt absurd, like why I am still grieving my siblings, my father and especially my brother, Owen, when they'd died so long ago.

IN THESE INTENSE GRIEVING MOMENTS, my solace was energy healing sessions, the singing bowls, the drums and rattles, the prayers and meditation. Though my limbs were, in a sense, reeling as the pain seared through my cells. Yet, I could release some fears and frustration, as I had the courage to touch and grip my pain.

I realised many things during therapy. Some not obvious while I was in a session, but that would emerge during reflection on my walks or while writing. I learned to turn down the volume of my anxiety, explore my fears and confront them. Also, as Geoff so often reminded me, I was able to be brutal in confronting the fears.

One of the major things I became aware of as my mind settled, was that I no longer had to prove myself to myself. A simple fact that for most would come easily. For me a constant battle with the oppressor to control my life, my mind, had eroded my confidence and, at the same time, made me determined to shine wherever I could. I had an obsessive need to assert control, to show others that I was as good as they seemed to be. Even after leaving South Africa and starting a new life in a free society, those thoughts inhibited my self-worth. I remained conditioned to look for signs of racism. It was an alertness, a vigilance that helped prevent an erosion of my spirit.

My first day home alone, after three months in therapy was a bigger mental challenge than I envisaged. I'd been preparing; I had my strategies in place. Bread flour, yeast and other ingredients gathered in readiness. I had been struggling with bouts of nausea and dry mouth.

I was carefully planning my route to the hospital for a scheduled appointment with the haematologist to check on my DVT.

'Make sure you leave early so you can find parking,' Chris reminded me when he called.

'Yes, of course, I will.'

'And if you feel that you can't drive, call me.'

'Will you stop worrying about me, I'll be fine.'

'I filled the car with petrol, so no need to stop on your way.'

'As always, my guardian angel on earth.'

'Just making sure that you will be OK.'

'I know and that's why I love you.'

DURING OUR HEALING SESSIONS, Geoff had paid special attention to the DVT and laid his hands on my leg, channelling healing energy while I meditated. When the specialist remarked that there was no trace of a DVT, considering that it may not have resolved since my last one, two years prior, I smiled. My openness and receptiveness to the healing sessions had brought good results.

My continued meditation practice had become my window to the beauty around me. Through the shamanic healing, the spirit world had become a comforting place. My firm belief in spirits, ancestors, guardian angels and a higher power, meant I could surrender to these energies during times of distress. My spirit could embrace them.

Therapy brought consolation — an acceptance and calm. It helped me to turn down the volume when the triggers surfaced. Trauma is, sadly, a part of life. Mine did not end as I had longed for. Yet, I continue to do all I can to change my mindset; continuously push myself towards progress.

Before I started working with Geoff, I thought counselling would be awkward, which left me hesitant to try it. The added financial stress of seeking psychological help was another reason to resist. I knew that many wounded souls walk among us unable to pay for private therapy and languishing on long hospital lists. The scariest part was knowing how to find a professional who I'd feel comfortable with.

During therapy, my trauma surfaced at the oddest times. Once, we were out for dinner and a waiter stumbled and dropped a full tray of drinks in my lap, there were four of us at the table so I instantly assumed the target had to be me. But I had a way to reset. I took a few moments to breathe and accepted it was an accident.

My ongoing tendency for accidents particularly after I'd worked so hard to get back on track, preyed on me. Every couple of weeks a new challenge presented itself and, I allowed them to erode my self-worth. When I was logical, I knew it was just part of life and something I should accept.

With the episodes came many surprises. Mostly in the form of amazingly, kind and supportive people. In June 2019, five weeks after my eye accident, I fell and crashed into a glass door. I tore my Achille's tendon. My head narrowly missed a metal pole as I fell into the glass door.

I was left unable to walk properly, and confined to the couch. It meant that for a time, I couldn't attend my therapy sessions. I panicked. Would my nightmares return?

Geoff arranged online sessions so we could continue. Doing meditation with him online helped lift my low mood as I struggled with the darkness around me.

The fall created another challenge to deal with just as I was about to start my first semester. If I hadn't been in therapy, I'd have seen it as a sure sign I was cursed. But instead of abandoning my studies, I was determined to keep going. I entered my first class in a moonboot.

I was treated by a local physiotherapist, Ben Marinozzi, whose care lifted my spirits. He provided exceptional support that was not only targeted at my physical healing but also my mental struggle. The timing of the accident was dire for another reason. I'd only recently regained the ability to drive; was looking forward to it on some level. But when the doctor cautioned against driving for at least three months, my mood sunk to a new low.

Ben pushed harder for me to succeed. He was a firm believer in natural healing therapies, including meditation and breathing techniques, so he devised my treatment plan and included a range of physical exercises. Whenever I felt frustrated with myself, my progress, he responded with empathy and kindness and after-hours support. When I finally shed the boot and walked unaided, he was as elated as I was. It left me in no doubt what a treasured practitioner he is.

'I've never worked with anyone as driven as you,' Geoff said. Ironically, it was at the same time that Chris was driving me to classes!

'It's definitely an upbringing thing, but I lost it for a while,' I said. 'Until I started working with you.'

In general, I'm far more drawn to complementary medicine and ancient healing methods and will always explore those first. I'm not recommending this as the only or, even, first method. It wouldn't suit everyone. And I never ruled out medical intervention.

However, when a friend of mine, killed himself, I was shattered. We'd been in touch via email only a short time before he died. In his message he had asked me what I thought about the after-life and also if I believed in reincarnation. Because of his usual positivity, I didn't equate this sudden curiosity with his imminent death. When it was revealed that he had been taking anti-depressants, I became more convinced that medication is not always the solution.

DON'T GET ME WRONG, my healing journey was not plain sailing. Both Geoff and I suffered bouts of frustration with each other. His throwaway lines infuriated and challenged me, while my neuroticism must have been frustrating for him. And, it was our mutual respect that shone through. For a while I had lost faith in life around me, but once I settled into the therapy process my enthusiasm for life slowly returned. These sessions carried me through those difficult months where I took a few steps forward and without warning, many steps backwards.

Therapy is not a one-sided journey that ends after the session. It is a painful examination of self and takes a concerted effort to keep doing 'the work' both inner and outer. As a child, I had a tendency to observe how people acted, behaved — particularly the adults who were frequent visitors in our home. I even kept notes about what they did and the things they said. I was regularly reading what might be happening behind Geoff's answers, his body language. I was, in fact, reading far too much into things.

After one trying session, I got the distinct impression that

Geoff wanted to refer me to someone else. His facial expressions were not overly obvious, but I had a sense he was going to suggest our sessions were over. I was very worried, not only about how I would cope, but how my whole family would feel. They were all so proud of my progress. If I stopped, it would be a setback for me but would also impact our family dynamics. I shuddered at the thought of starting with a new practitioner, especially when I knew I'd made so much progress.

My self-talk included the advice to not walk away, to find common ground and try to be accommodating of those who were working to help me heal. Geoff found a way to ease my fears whenever this tension and awkwardness reared its head.

'Say, "I struggle to deal with issues such as …".' Geoff encouraged me to phrase things like that when my instinct was to avoid the issue by saying, 'I don't know'. These simple techniques helped me open up areas of trauma, long buried, festering underneath the surface.

From the many sessions, and the to-and-fro of the healing journey, I've learned that patience is not my strong point (not everyone shares my work pace or passion for life). I've learned how perfectionism inhibits my joy. These are certainly two big issues to work on and ways to make drastic changes in my life. Learning that putting myself first is not a flaw has been a valuable lesson of this journey. *Who do I take care of? Who am I a failing?* Learning, too, that there is no shame in being flawed. Perfectionism is a relic of the 1950s and has no place in our lives today.

I've come to understand how precious the skills and efforts of truly good health practitioners are. I'm particularly impressed with those who combine allopathic and complementary methods. We, their clients, place enormous demands on them. Those in the private and public health systems are called on to deal with a growing mental health crisis in so many realms, in Australia.

Committed practitioners — I'm talking about those who consistently work long hours, give so much more than is expected of them — often suffer burnout and their own health crises. They have to balance family, work and have a life outside their practice. I respect them deeply and know their precious gifts must be revered and treasured.

So, as I reset so many of my previous, unhelpful ways of viewing my life, I have gained a new sense of what I'd like to focus on for my future. For now, that focus is on university studies and on writing more books. It means I'm immersed in writing projects and reading, reading, reading. It's inspiring. And, as I get further motivated, my analytical skills develop, my writing develops and I'm closer and closer to my dreams being fulfilled. The dream of writing more.

Mostly, though, I feel that a life of true contentment is finally within my grasp.

CHAPTER SEVENTEEN
AND SO, IT IS

I learned that courage was not the absence of fear, but the triumph over it. The brave man is not he who does not feel afraid but he who conquers fear.

— Nelson Mandela

WRITING *A DARKER SHADE OF PALE* remains my major creative achievement but, sadly, also the cause of my psychological unravelling. Over time, I will continue to come to terms with reliving my past. My heart will heal; that much I know. And what I've understood is that healing does not mean the hurt, the anguish goes away but, rather, that the intensity will lessen over time.

Geoff Lyons was, at face value, someone from the opposite side of the spectrum from me. His life looked so different from mine. And yet, how fortunate I was to meet him. He became my healer.

It's said, often, that everyone has a story — some tougher and more challenging than others. I believe the biggest issue I have; indeed, we have as humans, is a tendency to be judgmental. My preconceived ideas about Geoff were unfounded and unfair. Learning about his adversity growing up and his determination to forge a career, left me questioning my spontaneous judgement of his privilege and other people's privilege. And yes, because we live in this society with all its complex levels of status, Geoff will almost always have an advantage over many, born in different countries, of different genders, from different family circumstances. However, that doesn't diminish the inspiration I get from him which increases the more I understand how he struggled to reach his goal.

My work with Geoff was exactly what I needed to repair my broken spirit. I know I'm not completely out of the woods, but it's deeply comforting to have a place to go to and a practitioner who offers clients the options they desire.

In his large treatment room, with its light-coloured carpet and white ceiling, sat a portable table. There, stretched out in a meditative state, is where I connected with my ancestors.

The combination of talk therapy and energy healing had brought much relief to my ailing spirit. For the first time in many years, or ever, I had a genuine optimism. Many times, I knew I was presenting with such deep pain that I urged Geoff not to give up on me. He didn't.

At home, Chris, Sasha and Michelin noticed the changes in me and they too, started relaxing. All three of them, however, responded differently. Chris, always on high alert, took a while to settle and accept that it was not a distressed phone call when my name popped up on his phone. Sasha, remained practical and calm, always in the wings to listen and support, often with much humour. Michelin, diplomatic, logical — frustratingly so at times — was always on the other side of the phone or in the event of my accident proneness, on his way to the hospital.

I have so much to be grateful for this year. My own little family is growing. We've welcomed another little girl, Mia into the fold. Chelsea, Charlotte, Joshua and Alexander bring me so much joy. Mum, at 89, remains my biggest inspiration. My remaining siblings and my nieces and nephews are all on their own life's journeys. Whenever we gather, I listen to their stories and think about how fortunate they are to live a life free of legislated racism. These stories will remind them that we and their ancestors lived a life unimaginable to them.

These days, when I'm writing at my desk or walking in the park, I feel surrounded by love and see real beauty. The air around me feels different, I now notice the sounds of the birds even amid the noise of traffic. Those dark, threatening shadows are banished. They're swept up in the earth's atmosphere, where I hope a radiant light will dissolve them.

There are many people, like me, walking around with the pain of various traumas. We are the wounded warriors. When horrible things happened to us as humans, it is normal to harbour feelings of hatred and bitterness and wanting revenge. These feelings are destructive. It can destroy us.

We live with a silence, a voice that cannot adequately articulate our pain. This stems from a silence passed onto us by our parents. In our home, my father — ever critical of the government's inhumane policies — remained silent about the impact on him. Mum's responsibility to raise six children, was greater than the everyday humiliations. That generation, in particular, accepted their fate shrouded in silence. It was somehow wrong to question our oppressors. Their fear rendered them powerless.

When Mum recently talked about a buried traumatic event that happened to her more than 70 years ago when apartheid was legislated. I felt her pain as she unleashed her anger at our oppressors. One day, when she was 18, she was on her way to catch the train to work, only to find the bridge at the railway station had been declared open to white people only. It had changed from one day to the next. 'We were herded like cattle down the railway line,' she said, 'to the train crossing, to get to the other platform.' She had never spoken about this incident until then.

For me in particular, letting go of my intense dislike of the privileged and their wealth, acquired at our disadvantage is something I must accept that I cannot change. It is easier to say that than to accept. I agree that life is too short to walk around with this wound I know that this is something that only I can change when the time is right. The signs are already there.

In my healing sessions, I found ways to detoxify and to purge this poison from my mind and body. I wanted so desperately to be victorious. I've experienced life changing moments and the ability to divulge and let go of deeply personal memories. The constant flow of Geoff's healing energy often gave me periods of respite that offered a sense of hope that I could overcome this trauma.

Many times, during energy healing sessions, I felt my mental trauma subsiding which allowed me to talk about the hurtful memories buried under my scars.

'Do you know that while I was at college and working in a part-time job, relevant to the story, a white student told me that he would never marry outside his race because it would tarnish his bloodline.'

'Are you serious?' said Geoff.

'Yes,' I remember every detail of our conversation.'

'How did that make you feel?'

'I'd rather not answer.'

'Understood.'

I had so much unfinished business from my childhood. 'Trauma' comes from the Greek word for 'wound'; it's a wound that manifests in many ways. It is often described as a loss of feeling. My response to trauma fluctuates, from rage to self-loathing. Emotionally wounded people walk around with invisible wounds. It races around in our minds, fills our cells, tears us apart.

The more I talk about my pain and share this with others, the more a sense of belonging emerges. We have all been traumatised to some extent and it's important to find our tribe. We need a community to stand together; develop a camaraderie, a bond as survivors of a horrific period. There is no perfect group of people. We are all bound together on this journey. For us to be healers of others, we must first be healed.

The main elements that helped me work towards acceptance that my life is as it should be, and heal, were the many encouraging messages and reviews from readers, family and friends. Add to that, a healer with whom I could connect and believed in.

The beautiful people in this world allow us many opportunities to live as one family, with an immense capacity to love and be loved, to be kind amidst the horror, to share our life journey with all its perils and beauty. An important contributor to healing is the acknowledgement from a community of the hurts of the past. True healing begins when the wrongs are owned by those who committed the atrocities.

I won't easily forget the framed images of angel wings and luminous light in Geoff's healing room. Nor can I fully convey the joy of the tingling feeling or energy surging during one of his treatments. It is something marvellous, something to be experienced. It's a healing journey I can truly describe as life-altering.

My wish is that everyone walking around with pain and trauma gets the help they need. For there are many healers among us who can rise to the challenge to free us from pain. They live among us. Find them - - it will change your life.

ABOUT THE AUTHOR

Beryl Crosher-Segers is the author of *A Darker Shade of Pale*, a bestselling South African memoir about life during apartheid. In her writing debut she tells the story of her determination to rise above her earlier life of inequality and injustice.

Beryl and her husband moved to Australia in the 1980s in search of a better life for themselves and their children.

Through a long held love of the arts, she established One World Community Arts Network, a community project celebrating cultural diversity through music. In 2002, her commitment to previously disadvantaged artists from her birth town, led her to starting her own events company, C Major Events. Beryl's previous experience is in administration in government. She is also impassioned by fundraising.

A highly-regarded community representative, her awards include the Celebrate Africa–Australian Captain's Award for service to the South African Community and a Jo Wilton Memorial for Women, human rights award, from the University of Technology, Sydney.

Beryl is currently completing postgraduate studies in creative writing and writing her third book. She lives in Sydney, on the east coast of Australia, with her husband, daughter, son, daughter-in-law and grandchildren.

Beryl is available for presentations, workshops, live events, conferences, gatherings and book-signings.

WHERE TO FIND HELP

I recommend the following resources as a starting point to find help and guidance if you're in an anxious space, having panic attacks or experiencing any conditions I write about.

It's useful to talk to your general practitioner who can refer you to a mental-health practitioner.

IN AUSTRALIA

Lifeline: 24-hour crisis support
13 11 14 | http://www.lifeline.org.au

Suicide Prevention Australia
1300 659 467 | http://www.suicidepreventionaust.org

Beyond Blue
1300 224 636 | http:/www.beyondblue.org.au

Black Dog Institute
(02) 9382 2991 | http://blackdoginstitute.org.au

SANE Australia
1800 187 263 | https://www.sane.org